The Hamptons & Long Island Homegrown Cookbook

Local Food, Local Restaurants, Local Recipes

By Leeann Lavin

Photography by Lindsay Morris and Jennifer Calais Smith

Voyageur Press

Contents

The Hamptons & South Fork

The North Fork
& Shelter Island

The North Shore

The South Shore

Foreword

A decade or so ago, when my wife and I decided to move to the East End, it was partly the landscape that drew us. Here, a mere one hundred miles east of New York City, were rich, expansive farm fields being worked by farmers and their machines, dotted with potato barns and wineries and clusters of salad-growing greenhouses.

The major roads—Highway 27 on the South Fork and Route 25 on the North Fork—are laid out like arteries of gastronomic exploration, with farmstands and tasting rooms every hundred yards or so in the denser stretches. Miraculously, the whole region is closely bordered by a salty shoreline, our entire climate insulated by the heat-holding bays and oceans.

It's a landscape that dazzled us partly by what it yields. All manner of vegetables—potatoes and cauliflower are still big crops—erupt from ocean-tempered fields that enjoy one of the longest growing seasons in the region. East End fields regularly hold tomatoes, eggplants, and other summer hangers-on—even on Thanksgiving. Along the shore are clams and oysters and schools of fish that come close enough for casters or seiners. In deeper waters, Long Island fishers scoop up squid and flounder, porgies and herring.

I was glad to become a new part of the long history of farmers, fishers, poets, and happy eaters moved by freshly dug steamers, ears of sweet corn still warm from the field, Long Island duck, and the East End's blissful and complete culinary experience.

But what might have felt like a revolution ten years ago now feels like a full-blown renaissance. There is an established wine country with product sipped locally, in New York City and beyond, and deep-rooted vines have become an essential piece of the farmland preservation puzzle. The chefs who helped build Long Island cuisine are tweaking that puzzle, perhaps egged on by the eruption of home-grown Latino cooking.

Food entrepreneurs are everywhere—from cupcake makers to farm-to-table canners. Farmers' markets have sprouted up in virtually every town on the South Fork, while school districts from Riverhead to East Hampton are erecting greenhouses, upgrading their food, and leading farmer-focused field trips. Nano-breweries and distilleries are flourishing, and neighbors are rediscovering kitchen gardens and backyard poultry. While the East End has historically been the breadbasket of New York City, it's now reclaiming its role as the breadbasket for itself.

If it was the abundant harvest that first drew me to this area, then it was the constellation of farmers, fishers, winemakers, chefs, bakers, cheesemakers, beekeepers, and other people behind that harvest that caused me to stay. Yes, food fresh from the field is wondrous. But it's even more satisfying when you know the people and story behind it. Celebrating that story is the mission of *Edible East End*. It's a mission all of us share with this book. No matter what your role in the food chain is, I hope you consider these pages a call to action to know, savor, and support the people who feed all of us.

Brian Halweil
Editor, *Edible East End*
Sag Harbor, New York
April 2011

Introduction

It's no coincidence—though perhaps it can be considered a culinary manifest destiny—that the East End of Long Island has long been affectionately known as the Twin Forks. Today, the North and South Forks' twin tines can readily dish up the island's unparalleled farm-to-plate food experience.

Long Island is, in fact, the longest and largest island in the contiguous United States, extending nearly 120 miles from New York Harbor to Montauk Point, brimming with backwoods, farms, bays, and beaches. F. Scott Fitzgerald, while living on Long Island's Gold Coast, captured its character in the *Great Gatsby* as "that slender riotous island."

Home to America's first successful suburban expansion following World War II, it has also long been renowned for its affluence, ranked among the wealthiest counties in the country. Gilded Age mansions line the North Shore, *Architectural Digest* cover shots pay homage to Hollywood East on the South Fork in the Hamptons, and Wall Street financiers have long canoodled here with great artists and other famous residents, such as Jackson Pollack, Walt Whitman, Steven Spielberg, Martha Stewart, Donna Karan, Billy Joel, and Alec Baldwin. Weekenders from Manhattan ("the City") seek solace and rejuvenation at their Long Island country houses, and the undeniable source of that inspiration has always been Long Island's unique natural beauty and bounty.

Long before the island became the wealthy vacation mecca it is now, the native Shinnecock Indian tribe hunted, fished, and farmed on Long Island and taught the first European settlers how to do so—growing beans, foraging for wild plants, and using fish for fertilizer.

Farming became the island's first industry. Today, potato pastures may have given way to orchards and vineyards, and dairy and goat farms may have replaced the heritage duck's grass fields, but Long Island is still recognized as the most productive farming area in New York State.

The Island's tableau and its cultural heritage of homegrown agriculture have inspired a cadre of ingredients-minded master chefs who possess a reverence for their local food source. They have studied and cooked in renowned four-star restaurants across the island, from the Gold Coast to Hampton Bays, and all over the world. Regardless of whether the chefs relocated to discover the charms of the island or left briefly to pursue the siren song of culinary education elsewhere, or couldn't ever bear to leave, all feel the yearning for their *terroir*: Long Island.

The Hamptons and Long Island Homegrown Cookbook pays tribute to the remarkable, authentic farms, gardens, vineyards, and waterways that are Long Island. It also honors those chefs who are bringing Long Island's unique homegrown harvest to food-obsessed plates and palates and, in the process, helping the island's growers and food artisans preserve a precious way of life. Through their ardent beliefs, tenacity, and commitment to their craft and distinctive local cuisine, the chefs featured here have demonstrated a fidelity to the amazingly good, farm-forward Long Island cuisine.

The Hamptons and South Fork

Split at Riverhead from the North Fork, the South Fork peninsula is surrounded by water and encompasses the area commonly referred to as "The Hamptons," a lifestyle featured in the country's most haute society pages. Ask homeowners or visitors in the area what they like about it, and they'll rhapsodize about the beaches, surfing, fishing, wildlife, art, shopping, celebrity spotting, nightlife, and food.

Nick and Toni's

Chef Joseph Realmuto
Nick and Toni's Garden with Peconic Land Trust

There is perhaps no better example of the nexus of kitchen, garden, and fine art than Nick & Toni's restaurant in East Hampton, Long Island. Launched more than twenty years ago as the love child of husband-and-wife team Jeff Salaway and Toni Ross, Nick & Toni's has been a phenomenal success from the start. The two Manhattan restaurateurs were also acclaimed fine artists and avowed environmentalists with an unfailing commitment to local foods and the culinary arts. The dining rooms and terraces at Nick & Toni's are graced with fine art, and the menu illustrates their commitment to keeping local food on the plates.

Four years after they launched the restaurant, the owners invited gardening instructor Scott Chaskey from Quail Hill Farm, a stewardship project of the Peconic Land Trust, and his team of farmers and horticulturalists to lend their expertise to the restaurant's on-site kitchen garden. It took four more years to carve out the garden, Chaskey recalls. Today, he and his team use cover crops and religiously add four tons of compost every year.

Delineating the edge of the garden are sculptures by Salaway, who died in a car accident in 2001. His artistic works serve as the perfect transition between the garden's picturesque fruits and vegetables and the culinary art Chef Joe Realmuto creates in the kitchen. Having worked at Nick & Toni's for nearly twenty years, Joe has grown up steeped in the owners' farm-to-table credo and follows it in his menus.

Recognizing the ongoing influence he can exert on the local-food movement, Joe invests his time and talents in a number of education-based outreach efforts, including one-on-one conversations with customers, staff training, in-school gardening and cooking programs for students and their teachers, and sponsorship of community events.

Joe works closely with Chaskey and his team to plan the season's succession of plantings in the restaurant's garden. Introducing new and different varieties of foods adds interest to the growing season.

"We usually repeat a lot of things from one year to the next, but part of the joy of the garden is discovering these new things and figuring out what to do with them," Joe says.

He describes with relish the year he and his chefs were picking vegetables in the garden and spotted some knobby-looking items.

"They looked like orange zebra-striped heirloom tomatoes," Joe says. The chefs had no idea what they were. Turns out they were Turkish heirloom eggplants. "Freaky but delicious!" he says.

Chaskey echoes the chef's sentiment about finding new foods: "Farming is a lot of tractoring and hoeing. Part of our joy is discovering and growing new and exciting plant varieties."

The intensive staff training at Nick & Toni's ensures that the front line servers are well informed about the in-season, fresh foods on the menu. Daily staff meetings include sampling the day's menu additions. At the end of the session, everyone—from the busboy to the waiters—is expected not only to recite the menu but also be able to explain where the foods originated.

Joe came to cooking by way of his cultural heritage. Part of a happy Italian family that celebrated food, Joe and his siblings worked at the Villa Russo, a local Italian catering hall in Queens, where they grew up. His first job there was running food from the kitchen to the buffet table. Later, at age sixteen, he nabbed an opportunity to work in the kitchen. He worked every night after school, prepping for the weekend events; on Saturday and Sunday he worked doubles prepping for the catering-hall parties. He hung out with the chefs, who tempered his outlook about food and his career.

After graduating from the prestigious Culinary Institute of America (CIA) in 1993, he worked briefly at the River Café in New York City. Called "the Harvard Business School of the culinary world" and "the restaurant that launched a thousand chefs," the River Café was an ideal place to begin a career. It is also widely acknowledged as the first restaurant to seek out regional growers and artisanal food producers and build relationships with them (as opposed to "dialing and buying" in bulk from wholesale suppliers). In this environment, Joe was introduced to a nascent and emerging approach to fresher food resources.

When Joe started at Nick & Toni's in 1993, the prospects for local farmers were bleak. But with the new millennium came the new farm-to-table and Slow Food movements, and farms started to make a comeback, albeit in a different footprint.

The products from these local sources fit right in with Joe's "simple is better; simple is more" approach to cooking. He says, "I've always appreciated the product more than the technique. The biggest thing for me is freshness. It is the undeniable essence of flavor."

As Joe and his "family of farmers" think of the future, they look for ways to keep the farm-to-table movement going. The most important task now is helping local farmers fight the temptation to sell their farmland, which is worth so much more for development than it is for agriculture. Fortunately, local homeowners and the tourist industry recognize the importance of keeping Long Island farms alive.

And if Joe Realmuto has anything to do with it, they will succeed. Together, chefs like Joe and local farms in Long Island are connecting food and people in a meaningful and enduring way.

Garden Vegetable Agrodolce

Serves 8

3 medium eggplants, diced small

3 small green zucchini, quartered and cut into 1/4-inch pieces

3 small yellow squash, quartered and cut into 1/4-inch pieces

2 leeks, cut into 1/4-inch pieces

1 head fennel, cut into 1/4-inch slices

4 small garden peppers, cut in half and diced (any sweet variety of peppers, including red and yellow bell peppers or green Italian Cunanelle peppers—whatever is homegrown and seasonal)

4 large garden tomatoes, chopped

1 1/2 c. extra virgin olive oil, divided

salt and fresh black pepper, to taste

1 1/2 c. red wine vinegar

2 tbsp. sugar

3 cloves garlic, thinly sliced

1 c. kalamata olives, pitted and chopped

1 c. capers

1 c. prepared house-made tomato sauce

2 tbsp. fresh parsley leaves, chopped

2 tbsp. fresh oregano leaves, chopped

Preheat the oven to 500 degrees. In a bowl, toss the eggplant, zucchini, yellow squash, leeks, fennel, peppers, and tomatoes with 3/4 c. olive oil and season it with salt and pepper. Spread the vegetables on a cookie sheet in an even layer; cook for 8 to 10 minutes, or until the vegetables are cooked through and slightly browned. (*Chef's note:* At Nick and Toni's, we have the luxury of cooking the vegetables in a wood-fired oven, which adds a layer of smoke to the vegetables that is spectacular.)

To make the agrodolce: Combine the red wine vinegar and sugar in a small saucepan; cook over medium-high heat for 3 to 4 minutes, or until the liquid is reduced by half.

In a heavy-bottomed saucepan, warm the remaining 3/4 c. olive oil and sauté the garlic until golden brown. Add the roasted vegetables, olives, capers, tomato sauce, fresh herbs, and agrodolce. Season with a pinch more salt and pepper, and cook for an additional 5 minutes. Serve with your favorite piece of fish or as an antipasto.

Peconic Bay Scallops with Butter and Lemon over Garden Arugula

Serves 4

We also make this same dish with the addition of 1 lb. spaghetti. It is made the same way, but we add the arugula to the pan to slightly wilt it and then toss it with pasta.

2 bunches arugula
1 tbsp. olive oil
2 tbsp. unsalted butter, divided
1 lb. Peconic Bay scallops
juice of 2 lemons
salt and pepper, to taste
1 c. croutons, crushed

Clean the arugula, and place it on a platter.

Heat a large, thick-bottomed sauté pan over high heat. Add oil and 1 tbsp. butter to the pan and wait until it starts to smoke. It is very important that the pan be hot, or the scallops will stick to the pan and not brown.

Add scallops to the pan in an even layer and let them sit for 1 minute. Do not touch the scallops until they start to brown. Shake the pan to turn and brown the scallops on all sides. This should take no more then 2 minutes; it is better for the scallops to be a bit undercooked.

Add the lemon juice, remaining butter, and salt and pepper, and swirl the pan to just melt the butter. Once you have a nice, thick, buttery lemon vinaigrette, pour it over the arugula and top with crouton crumbs. Serve warm.

Ribollita: Garden Cavalo Nero and Barloti Bean Soup

Serves 20

1/4 c. plus 3 tbsp. extra virgin olive oil
1/2 c. flat-leaf parsley leaves, chopped
1 head fennel, chopped
4 cloves garlic, chopped
3 carrots, chopped
1 onion, chopped
kosher salt and freshly ground black pepper
1 (28 oz.) can whole peeled tomatoes
2 lb. cavalo nero, trimmed and roughly chopped
1 lb. cooked barloti beans, drained
1 gal. plus 1/2 c. water
1 stale, crustless loaf ciabatta bread (about 3/4 lb. whole)
1 c. Parmesan cheese
extra virgin olive oil

Heat 1/4 c. of the oil in a pot over medium-high heat. Add parsley leaves, fennel, garlic, carrots, onion, and salt and pepper to taste. Cook, stirring, until light brown, 15 to 20 minutes.

Crush the tomatoes, and add them to the pot. Reduce the heat to medium-low; cook until thickened, 25 to 30 minutes. Add the cavalo nero, three-quarters of the cooked beans, and 1 gal. water. Cover; bring to a boil. Reduce the heat to medium-low; simmer, uncovered, until the cavalo nero is tender (about 30 minutes).

Meanwhile, purée the remaining quarter of the cooked beans and 1/2 c. water in a food processor. Stir the mixture into the pot. Tear bread into 1-inch pieces; add the pieces to the pot with the remaining 3 tbsp. olive oil, Parmesan cheese, and salt and pepper to taste. Cook, stirring, until thick (about 30 minutes). Serve drizzled with extra virgin olive oil.

East Hampton Grill
(Formerly Della Femina)

Chef Michael Rozzi
Balsam Farms

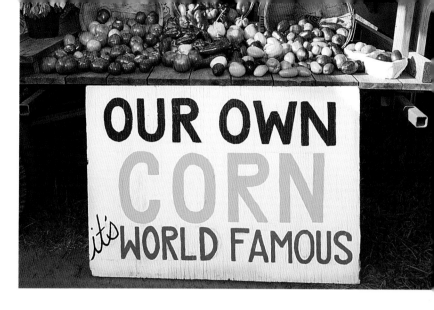

Though he's traveled a lot, Michael Rozzi, executive chef at the East Hampton (formerly Della Femina), says the most interesting place he's ever been is Long Island. He is a homegrown ambassador for the simple, healthy lifestyle he saw around him during his boyhood in the Hamptons. Although the decline of local farming had already begun during his childhood in the 1960s and 1970s, he still remembers that almost every local either worked in food gathering or producing or knew someone who did.

In earlier days, the food grown in the county stayed there, and people visited to enjoy that provenance. Today, Michael is re-creating that phenomenon by continually seeking out small growers who can offer his kitchen a variety of homegrown food.

"It was always my goal to do that here. My roots are here, and I've always been proud of our bounty. My garden is the East End of the Hamptons!" he says.

Since 1996, when he was first hired at Della Femina, Michael has been committed to using only domestically produced artisanal food. But he remembers he almost had to beg the farmers to work with him, because they could make more money selling their produce retail at their farmstands. He started with consistently buying their abundant "leftover" produce. Today, the restaurant has a lot of farmer friends, and Michael's network of artisanal partners also includes fishermen, butchers, and the "cheese guy."

Michael believes that even before the first bite, food has to make a visual statement, and he couldn't have a better setting for his dining-as-art presentations. The East Hampton Grill's walls are lined with graphic-art portraits featuring some of the restaurant's more storied customers and clients.

Michael grew up enjoying a simple, outdoor life that included hunting, horseback riding, fishing, and cooking with fresh vegetables grown in the family's own big yard. He always knew he'd become a chef, and he grew up in a family of good cooks.

Knowing he had a knack for cooking, he went to trade school for two years after high school. For several summers, he was a "spectator to the culinary and restaurant culture." He chopped vegetables and washed dishes for several great Hamptons restaurants, including the Deck, where he witnessed a superior level of culinary sophistication and learned how a cooking brigade works in sync to turn out great food consistently.

One of his fondest early restaurant experiences was working for Al and Mary Veltman at their popular restaurant Fishnet. Al caught the fish and seafood, and Mary selected fresh local produce from the farmstand. They gave Michael his start cooking local cuisine, teaching him how to get the best from fresh, local ingredients by not doing too much to them and instead just preserving their pure taste and flavors.

"If there are too many ingredients, the customers can't identify and enjoy what they are eating," he explains.

After receiving his culinary arts degree from Johnson & Wales in Providence, Rhode Island, Michael began his apprenticeship with Chef Bernard Miny at his diminutive restaurant, Le Chef. In the five years he worked at Le Chef, Michael learned basic French cooking and managing techniques and gained a sincere respect for the ingredients and the culture of his coworkers.

Though the East End is his garden, Michael defines "local" as "regional." He'll use squid from Rhode Island, which isn't that far from Montauk, and cheese and produce from the Hudson Valley. This sense of place and the emphasis on an area's unique food drives his culinary style, which is essentially country comfort food with a twist.

Michael also says he purposely seeks out "the small guys," such as Balsam Farms, the sixty-acre produce farm located in the high rent area of East Hampton. Owners Alex Balsam and Ian Calder-Piedmonte grow just enough for local chefs, farmers' markets, and their own Balsam farmstand.

"Their names are not on the boxes; they don't have a fleet of big trucks—just an old red pickup," Michael says with a grin.

Alex, the attorney, and on-site farmer and former philosophy major Ian lease and rent seven fields in the Hamptons and are part of East End Community Organic Farm (ECCO) of Long Island. They emphasize quality produce and hard-to-find vegetables. "We were farmstand kids," says Ian, referring to his grandfather's Vermont dairy farm and his involvement in the state's first soybean crop.

Michael uses the term "field heat" to describe just how fresh the vegetables and fruits from Balsam are: "I can still feel the warmth of the sun on the just picked food! It's very exciting to hold the living food in your hand," he enthuses.

It's also important to teach customers about eating with the seasons, says Michael. "Sure, they'd like a basil and tomato salad in December, but that's just not realistic," he says. Instead, diners get sea bass only when the sea bass fishing season opens in June, and tomatoes are available only in the summer.

"The important thing is using food you love and to offer a choice," he says.

Local Corn and Clam Chowder

Serves 4–6

4–6 oz. sweet sausage, loose
1 clove garlic, peeled and chopped
1/2 c. celery, diced medium
1/2 c. onion, diced medium
1/2 c. carrots, peeled and diced medium
2–3 tbsp. olive oil
2 tbsp. flour
1 c. white wine
2 c. clam juice
2 c. whole milk
1/2 c. potatoes, diced medium
1 c. fresh corn kernels
1 c. fresh clams, minced
1/2 tsp. paprika
1/2 tsp. turmeric
salt and pepper, to taste
1 tbsp. parsley, chopped
1 tsp. chives, chopped
1 tsp. freshly picked thyme

In a Dutch oven, over medium-high heat, cook the sausage until it begins to turn brown. Add garlic, celery, onion, carrots, and olive oil. Sauté the vegetables until they begin to soften. Add the flour, and stir to coat the vegetables.

Slowly add white wine and then allow to cook, reducing the wine by half. Add the clam juice, milk, potatoes, corn, clams, paprika, turmeric, and salt and pepper. Stir, then reduce the heat to low and simmer. Cook until the potatoes are tender (about 20 minutes). Add fresh herbs, and season to taste.

Salad of Local Beets and Apples
with Preserved Cherries and Fennel

Serves 4–6

- **3 large red beets, or 2–3 bunches baby beets**
- **1/3 c. red wine vinegar**
- **1 c. extra virgin olive oil**
- **1/4 c. whole-grain mustard**
- **3 tbsp. honey**
- **2 tsp. fresh mint, chopped**
- **salt and pepper, to taste**
- **1/2 c. dried cherries**
- **1 large apple, sliced**
- **2 bulbs fresh fennel, trimmed, washed, and shaved or sliced thinly**
- **3 oz. toasted hazelnuts, chopped**

Roast the beets in a 375-degree oven until they are tender enough for a knife to be easily inserted into their centers (approximately 30 minutes). Cool, peel, and cut the beets into bite-sized pieces.

While the beets are cooking and cooling, whisk together the vinegar, olive oil, mustard, honey, and mint in a small bowl. Season the vinaigrette with salt and pepper to taste, and set aside.

In a separate bowl, plump the cherries with warm or acidulated water, and set them aside. After draining the cherries, place them in a mixing bowl with the apple, fennel, and beets. Spoon the vinaigrette over the salad, and lightly toss to coat. Season with salt and pepper; divide the salad evenly among the plates, and garnish each with toasted hazelnuts.

Pan-Roasted Montauk Striped Bass

Pan-Roasted Montauk Striped Bass

Serves 4

SUN GOLD TOMATO CRUDA AND WAX BEAN SALAD:

3 pt. Sun Gold cherry tomatoes
1/3 c. sherry vinegar
1 c. extra virgin olive oil
1 large shallot, peeled
salt and pepper, to taste
4 tbsp. flat parsley, chopped
2 tbsp. fresh oregano, chopped
1/2 c. chives, chopped
3 c. tricolored wax beans, cut in half on a bias

In a blender, combine 2 pt. of the cherry tomatoes, sherry vinegar, olive oil, and shallot, and blend for 1 to 2 minutes until smooth. Season with salt and pepper to taste. Set aside.

Cut the remaining cherry tomatoes into halves in a separate bowl, and add the chopped parsley, oregano, chives, and blended tomato dressing.

In a boiling pot of salted water, cook the beans approximately 1 to 2 minutes until they are crisp-tender; drain and then shock them in a small bowl of ice water. When cooled, remove the beans from the ice water and pat them dry with a clean towel.

Add the beans to the tomato and herb mixture, mix lightly, and set aside.

HEIRLOOM ZUCCHINI AND SUMMER SQUASH GRATIN:

2 medium-sized green zucchini
2 medium-sized summer squash (summer yellow)
2 large shallots, peeled
6–8 tbsp. extra virgin olive oil
salt and pepper

Preheat the oven to 375 degrees. Using a Japanese mandolin, slice the zucchini, squash, and shallots into 1/8-inch-thick slices, keeping each in separate small bowls. Drizzle each with olive oil, and toss lightly to coat. Season with salt and pepper.

Line a baking pan with parchment paper. On the left side of the pan, create a column three slices wide, starting with a row of zucchini. Then add a row of yellow squash. Repeat the alternating rows down the length of the baking sheet. Create three more columns the same way, for a total of four individual-sized portions. Top each of the columns with the seasoned shallots.

Place the pan in the preheated oven and bake for 15 to 25 minutes, rotating the pan halfway through the baking time. After baking, loosely cover the pan with foil and keep it warm.

PAN-ROASTED BASS:

2–3 tbsp. extra virgin olive oil
4 striped bass filets, about 5–6 oz. each, skin on
salt and pepper

Preheat the oven to 400 degrees. Heat a large, nonstick, oven-safe sauté pan on the stove on high heat. Allow the pan to heat, and then add olive oil. Season the fish filets with salt and pepper, and carefully place each filet skin side down into the pan. Cook for 2 to 3 minutes. Reduce the heat to low, and continue to cook the fish for 4 to 5 more minutes, until the skin begins to turn brown. Place the entire pan of fish in the oven for 5 to 8 minutes or until the flesh is cooked through, but not well done. Remove the fish from the oven, and set aside.

To serve: Using a spatula, remove the Heirloom Zucchini Summer Squash Gratin from the pan and place it on a dinner plate. Then place one Pan-Roasted Bass filet, skin side up, next to the gratin. Mix the Tomato Cruda sauce, and spoon it over the fish.

Loaves & Fishes

Chef Anna Pump
Loaves & Fishes Herb Garden

Anna Pump is the proverbial fairy godmother of the East. The East End, that is. Bestowing her gifts of pure and simple ingredients, her advice on entertaining, and her approach to enjoying life in the Hamptons on her business, she almost single-handedly crafted the sophisticated yet casual approach to dining and entertaining that is revered by weekenders, food fans, and Long Island locals. Her unique and often-imitated style receives so much respect simply because it is authentic.

In 1980, Anna bought the Hamptons Specialty Food Shop in Sagaponack and launched a gourmet takeout enterprise, Loaves & Fishes. Her grandchildren now work the shop with her, sweetly yet authoritatively dispensing such sage advice as, "Trust me on this, you will want to go with the chocolate-brownie cake," while customers contemplate the myriad dessert creations dazzling the jewelry store–like display cases.

A chef, baker, innkeeper, food and entertainment entrepreneur, cooking instructor, and community-food and health activist, Anna wrote the first of her four cookbooks, *Loaves and Fishes* (published in 1986) for the many friends and customers who liked her food and wanted to learn how to make her signature dishes for themselves.

How exactly did this matriarch of all things Hamptons come to preside over this tip of Long Island, a world away from her family's farm on the Danish-German border?

Anna and her husband immigrated to the United States after World War II, settling near the town of Stockton, New Jersey. By the 1960s, Anna was a young mother with two small children. Her innate interest in food led her to read gourmet magazines and cookbooks— and learn about her adopted country's culture. She didn't speak any English when she moved to America, so all that reading also helped her learn the language.

Before long, in a mark of culinary valor, she signed up to study cooking in New York City—with James Beard, whom the *New York Times* had declared to be "the dean of American cookery." He affirmed both her cooking prowess and her devotion to real, quality ingredients.

Sometime in the late 1970s, a friend offered Anna and her husband the use of a rental house in the Hamptons for two summer weekends. That first visit to the Hamptons struck her like a clarion call.

"It felt so right. I can never forget that it even *smelled* great. We loved the Hamptons right away," she remembers.

The area between the Baltic Sea and the North Sea where Anna grew up was known for its fishing and farming and, in Anna's way of thinking, is the geographical twin to the East End of Long Island. Her family's land was a working farm, meaning "every single square inch of [the farm's] precious forty acres yielded produce" at harvest time, she wrote in *Loaves and Fishes*. After harvesting and preparing the farm for winter, they would begin storing winter vegetables in the basement of the farmhouse; canning plums, apples, cherries, and pears; and gathering wheels of cheese, milk, and butter in another room.

"There was always a lot of cooking going on in our house," Anna recalls. "My mother could make something out of nothing—and everything started from scratch."

Anna brought her family's heritage of cooking, baking, and gardening with her to Long Island. A hallmark of Anna's cooking is her own inventiveness, and she cooks seasonally—just like her mother did. Anna also studied with Scotsman Maurice Margette, who ran a cooking school on Shelter Island, and with Ann Maria Husta, who cooked for the Kennedy White House. In 1979, her first summer in the Hamptons, she worked for Ina Garten, now known as the Barefoot Contessa, in Garten's little shop in West Hampton Beach.

Looking back, Anna remembers when she first opened the store, a farmer came and wanted to sell her eggs. She has been buying eggs from him ever since. Just down the road from her is Pike Farms in Sagaponack; she walks there on Monday morning and buys her produce, running a tab with farmer Jim Pike.

Anna describes how in early spring she picks ornamental pear tree branches for a bouquet to put in the store, and she is equally romantic and enthusiastic about her flowering cherries and chives. Her oregano, thyme, tarragon, sage, and lemon balm are grown next to the kitchen at the shop, and she also grows root celery, leeks, parsnips, and carrots.

At Loaves & Fishes, Anna changes her menu every week and posts the entire listing online. Inspired by the unending variety of fresh, homegrown ingredients, Anna has thousands of recipes in her repertoire.

"I always start with the ingredients—whatever is fresh. For instance, in spring ramps are so easy to broil or grill," she says. In the colder months, there is a world of stews, casseroles, and cassoulets to explore.

Lobster Potato Salad

Serves 6

Preparation time: 45 minutes
What could be a better combination than the simplest of foods served with the most sublime? The earthy potato and the succulent lobster, dotted with tangy capers, make a marvelous lunch.

  2 lb. small white potatoes
  3 c. lobster meat, cooked
  2/3 c. dill, chopped
  4 scallions, green parts only, chopped
  3 tbsp. capers in vinegar, drained
  2 tbsp. vinegar from the capers
  1 1/2 tbsp. lemon juice
  3/4 tsp. salt
  3/4 tsp. ground black pepper
  3/4 c. mayonnaise
  dill sprigs, for garnish

Boil the potatoes for 15 minutes, then drain. Let them stand until they are cool enough to handle, then cut them into bite-sized pieces. Place them in a large salad bowl. Cut the lobster into bite-sized pieces, and add that to the potatoes. Sprinkle with the dill, scallions, capers, caper vinegar, lemon juice, salt, and pepper. Finally, add the mayonnaise, and mix the salad gently with your hands, being careful not to break the potatoes. Garnish with dill sprigs.

Baked Seafood Sagaponack

Serves 8

Preparation time: 1 hour
A beautifully rich, wholesome, and authentic local dish, which takes less than an hour to prepare. Be sure to serve lots of warm, crusty Italian bread to soak up the delicious creamy tomato sauce.

SAUCE:
  2 tbsp. butter
  2 tbsp. olive oil
  1 1/2 c. onion, peeled and chopped
  1 c. leek (white parts only), diced
  1/2 c. fennel, chopped
  5 cloves garlic, peeled and minced
  3 lb. ripe tomatoes or drained canned tomatoes, chopped
  1 1/2 c. dry white wine
  1 1/2 c. chicken stock
  2 tbsp. chopped fresh basil, or 1 tsp. dried
  1 tbsp. chopped fresh thyme, or 1/2 tsp. dried
  1 tbsp. chopped fresh oregano, or 1 tsp. dried
  1/2 tsp. hot red pepper flakes
  salt and pepper, to taste
  1/2 c. heavy cream

Heat the butter and oil in a large, heavy, nonaluminum sauté pan. Add the onion, leek, and fennel. Sauté over low heat for about 5 minutes, stirring occasionally. Add the garlic, tomatoes, wine, and chicken stock, and bring the mixture to a boil. Lower the heat, and let it simmer. Add the basil, thyme, oregano, hot red pepper flakes, and salt and pepper. Cover the pan, and simmer for 20 minutes. Remove the cover and simmer for 5 minutes more. Add the cream. Increase the heat to high for 5 minutes to reduce the sauce. Remove from the heat, and let cool slightly.

SEAFOOD:
  3 lb. filet of anglerfish, tilefish, or any firm-fleshed fish
  1 lb. raw shrimp, shelled
  2 whole lobsters, cut into serving-sized pieces
  2 doz. mussels, scrubbed and steamed open, for garnish
  1/2 c. capers, drained, for garnish
  chopped parsley, for garnish

Preheat the oven to 375 degrees. Pour half the sauce into a large, shallow baking dish. Add all the fish, except for the mussels. Pour the remaining sauce over the fish. Bring to a simmer on top of the stove. Cover with a piece of buttered parchment paper, buttered side down, and bake for 10 to 12 minutes. Remove from the oven. Discard the paper, and garnish with the mussels, capers, and parsley.

Zucchini-Pepper Soup

Serves 8

Preparation time: 50 minutes
A delicate green color and a smooth, refreshing vegetable taste make this a perfect first course. It can be served hot or chilled and goes very well with almost any main course.

SOUP:

4 small zucchini, cut into 1/2-inch pieces

2 green peppers, seeded and coarsely chopped

1 1/2 c. onion, peeled and coarsely chopped

4 c. chicken stock

1 1/2 c. sour cream

4 sprigs parsley, leaves only, chopped

1 tsp. salt

1/2 tsp. ground black pepper

Place the zucchini, peppers, onion, and chicken stock in a saucepan, and bring to a boil. Reduce the heat, and allow it to simmer for 15 minutes. Remove from the heat, and let cool for 15 minutes. Pour half the soup mixture and half the sour cream into the bowl of a food processor fitted with a metal blade. Add the parsley, salt, and pepper. Whirl until smooth. Add the rest of the ingredients, and process until smooth.

TO SERVE:

1 small zucchini, thinly sliced

1/2 c. sour cream

8 sprigs dill

Serve soup in bowls topped with a slice of zucchini, a dollop of sour cream, and a sprig of fresh dill.

The American Hotel

Chef Jonathan Parker (left), Owner Ted Conklin (right)
The American Hotel Garden

When Ted Conklin was introduced to the building that would become the American Hotel, it was sagging from the burden of lost potential. Yet Ted, a visionary, businessman, and former gentleman farmer, saw something else: a center for the community.

Buying the former stagecoach inn in 1971, he got right to work. He spent the better part of the winter fixing up the main part of the hotel and was ready to open it for guests by the spring tourist season of 1972. Today, there is a friendly ambiance in the wood paneling, the floors that creak at just the right note, and a décor that must surely inspire Ralph Lauren's boutique designers with its all-American exuberance.

And the hotel is indeed a meeting place. The American Hotel in Sag Harbor has become a warm, inviting home away from home for locals, tourists, and celebrities like musicians Billy Joel and Jimmy Buffet, artists Dan Rizzie and Eric Fishl, writers Bob Caro and Thomas Harris, actors Alec Baldwin and Lauren Bacall, and business luminaries Ken Chenault and Dick Grasso. Families reserve tables at the hotel for holiday Christmas dinners or other special occasions. Farmers, vineyard owners, and public servants convene here for lively discussions, Ted's hospitality, and good, farm-fresh, local food prepared and presented in a sophisticated way by executive chef Jonathan Parker.

Jonathan spent a lot of his youth in Devon (southwestern England) cooking "solid English food" with his grandmother and working in local restaurants. He later completed a two-year cooking program before moving to London to work at St. James in the boutique Hotel Hempstead, under a maniacal, yelling, stomping French chef. From there, he joined the kitchen of another French chef, Bernard Gaume, at the Carlton Towers in Knightsbridge. Gaume introduced him—and their London dining guests—to fantastic imported French ingredients.

Wanting to continue to expand his culinary craft, Jonathan signed on to work as a saucier chef in L'Hotel Majestic in the south of France for two years. There, farmers brought him three-wheeled wagons filled with exquisite chanterelles or leeks. Fishermen from the Cote d'Azur brought a kaleidoscope of fresh-caught fish. It was a fortuitous assignment for many reasons: He learned to speak fluent French, was in charge of a staff of six people, and met his wife, who hailed from Long Island. It was love and marriage that brought him to the United States.

Here he landed a hat trick of plum cooking jobs, working at Le Reserve and Rafael with Thomas Keller and at Le Bernadin with Eberhard Müller. Once established in New York's culinary constellation, he became executive chef at the Ocean Club, where he won rave reviews for fourteen years and led the move to use local fish rather than what French-trained cuisine had demanded.

After September 11, 2001, Jonathan and his wife sought a change. They moved to San Antonio, Texas, and he took up the reins as executive chef at the seafood restaurant Pesca. But after a few years, they returned to the water and his wife's family homestead on Long Island, where he began cooking for Ted's American Hotel.

Many of the ingredients for Jonathan's creative dishes come directly from Ted's garden, located a few short blocks away from the hotel. The garden serves up asparagus, tomatoes, and plentiful herbs for the chef's inspiration and the dining guests' delight.

It shouldn't be a surprise that the American Hotel has become a destination for both locavores and visitors wanting to taste Long Island's terroir. Ted's long track record of successful enterprises extends back to establishing and running a restaurant while he was still in college. After graduation, he bought 200 acres just off Lake Ontario and raised livestock and vegetables for two years before returning to his native Long Island to renovate the American Hotel and establish North American Farm, which for five years supplied the American Hotel with fresh ingredients.

After Ted sold that farm and bought a restored Tuscan farmhouse as his vacation home, he became aware of a burgeoning initiative called the Slow Food movement. Intrigued by and definitely supportive of the group's mission, Ted returned to the United States and launched the East End chapter. For more than a dozen years, the American Hotel hosted the Slow Food East End dinners, and Ted served as chapter leader.

Ted does not see embracing local food, farming, and edible gardens as a trend, but as an enduring commitment to what matters most. In keeping with that commitment, his home kitchen garden is cultivated solely for the restaurant. The beautiful garden, about a quarter of an acre in size, was laid out by Ted and local horticulture expert Peter Garnham, who also helps maintain it. Neat rows of asparagus, arugula, tomatoes, kale, and a variety of fragrant herbs form an edible landscape that is the basis for the hotel's menu.

Jonathan says the garden produce's just-picked taste and fragrances are extraordinary inspiration for his culinary art. Every week, he consults the gardeners to see what is ready to be harvested and plans his cooking accordingly.

Using local food is more work, he notes, because "it's not prewashed and cut. It takes time to organize and sort." But as Ted Conklin, his fellow Slow Food enthusiasts, and the clientele at the American Hotel can all attest, it is worth the effort.

Peconic Clam Chowder

Serves 8

1 c. smoked bacon, finely diced
1/2 lb. sweet butter
2 medium onions, chopped to 1/4-inch dice
4 c. leeks, whites only, washed and chopped to 1/4-inch dice
1 bouquet garni (2 fresh bay leaves, 3 sprigs fresh thyme, and
  6 fresh parsley stalks tied together)
1 c. dry white wine
2 c. Wondra flour
2 qt. clam juice, heated and strained
1 qt. milk, hot
1 qt. cream, hot
3 c. Yukon Gold potatoes, peeled and diced small
1/2 gal. chowder clams, chopped and juice reserved
1 qt. surf clams, chopped
salt and pepper, to taste
3 tbsp. fresh parsley, chopped

In a stockpot, render down the bacon until it is light golden brown. Add and melt the butter. Add the onions, leeks, and bouquet garni. Sweat, covered, for 10 minutes (cook gently with a lid on low-medium to low heat). Deglaze with the white wine, and on a low flame, reduce until dry. Add the flour and cook, stirring for 5 minutes, to form a blonde roux.

Gradually add in the hot clam juice, milk, and cream, and any strained juices from the clams. Stir. Add the potatoes, and cook until they are cooked but still a little firm (about 15 minutes). Next, add both chowder clams and surf clams. Simmer for 10 minutes. Stir well, and skim off any impurities. Add salt and pepper to taste and chopped parsley. Serve immediately with crusty bread.

Croque Monsieur

Serves 1

2 tbsp. béchamel sauce
2 slices white sandwich bread, crusts removed
4 slices Gruyere cheese
3 oz. good boiled ham, sliced
pepper, to taste (optional)
4 tbsp. sweet butter

Preheat the oven to 350 degrees. Spread the béchamel on the bread slices. Place one slice of cheese on top of each bread slice. Divide the ham between the bread slices. Season very lightly with black pepper, if desired.

In a sauté pan over low heat, add the butter until it starts to foam. Place the topped bread slices into the pan, and slip the pan into the oven for 5 minutes, just until the sandwich is golden, the cheese has melted, and the ham is hot. Take the pan out of the oven and place the two pieces together to form a sandwich. Cut it in half diagonally before serving.

Serve with coleslaw, a potato salad, or crisp, mixed field greens.

Baked Apples Bonne Maman

Serves 4

4 Honey Crisp apples
4 tbsp. golden raisins
8 tbsp. butter
1 tsp. vanilla extract
4 tbsp. light brown sugar
1 tbsp. honey
2 c. fresh apple juice

Preheat the oven to 350 degrees. Cut off the tops of the apples. Core the apples, and score skin around the middle circumference of the apples. Stuff 1 tbsp. raisins into each apple center, and replace the apple top. Place the stuffed apples into a suitable roasting pan.

Meanwhile, in a saucepan, melt the butter. Stir in the vanilla, brown sugar, and honey. Stir in the apple juice. Pour the mixture over the apples and bake for 50 minutes, basting every 15 minutes. Remove the pan from the oven, then the apples from the pan before reducing the juices to a glaze. Pour the glaze over the apples, and serve warm with vanilla ice cream.

Almond

Chef Jason Weiner

Pike Farms

Jason Weiner's culinary career started with a dose of drama. Deciding to take a year's sabbatical from college, he answered a *New York Times* classified ad for a line chef. Though he had no previous formal culinary experience, he got the position—at Regine's on Park Avenue, a storied nightclub and dinner theater that hosted the likes of Liza Minnelli and Andy Warhol. When he showed up for work, he discovered his good fortune was a result of the union chefs being on strike, and he had to cross the picket line, where there was quite a bit of shouting. Once ensconced in the kitchen, he got a crash course in restaurant cooking.

"There was lots of screaming and yelling in the kitchen too," he says with a chuckle. On the other hand, there also was serious haute cuisine, and Jason started to learn classic French cooking techniques and sauce making from Frenchman Jean Claude. But the best part of the experience was Jason's discovery that he wanted a culinary career.

The following year, he moved on to the new China Grill in the CBS Black Rock building with its groundbreaking open kitchen and food-as-theater, and then relocated to San Francisco to help open Aqua restaurant in 1991. In 1998, the management asked him to open another Aqua in the Bellagio, Las Vegas, where he served as the executive sous chef for three years. In a place where glitter and showgirls are *de rigueur*, he prepared food that was applauded as theatrical, architectural cuisine. But he wanted to return to a place where the ingredients got top billing.

Looking back, he recognizes that he'd always embraced fresh food and pure ingredients as the basis of his cooking philosophy. His culinary instinct and eating preferences were nurtured by his Monday night dining rituals at Alice Waters' Chez Panisse, where for only $35, he could indulge in a three-course dining nirvana.

"Me and some of the other restaurant staff were strapped for cash, to be sure. Panisse was already the food temple—the shrine. And with that menu price, we ended up going there quite a bit and learning quite a lot," he says.

Jason eventually returned to the Hamptons, where he and Eric Lemonides, his childhood friend from Brooklyn, decided to start a restaurant together. They soon found an available spot for rent and opened Almond in the spring of 2001.

"While the Hamptons area is known for its celebrity lifestyle, we knew it was at the heart of the farming and fishing community, and we really wanted that heritage and tradition to continue," Jason says.

Jason eventually recognized the vast food opportunity in Long Island—especially in the growing season, when he gets a solid ninety percent of his products from within a ten-mile radius of the restaurant.

"I'm watching it come right out of the ground on the way to work," he says. "And that night I'm putting it on people's plates. It's incredibly rewarding."

The success of Almond restaurant on Long Island allowed Jason and Eric to open a second restaurant in New York City located near Union Square and its incredible Greenmarket. Jason has cultivated lasting relationships with the growers there, along with other food artisans.

"When we first opened Almond, it was me reaching out to the farmers, going to farmstands and starting conversations. Some of the farmers produced just enough for retail; it wasn't part of their business model to do anything else. And some could only do wholesale. Then there was a third group: folks who'd never thought about selling to the restaurants. They'd say, 'Let me think about that,'" Jason says. It sometimes took a year for them to get on board, but they'd call him back and say, "OK."

He shares a particularly close working relationship with a few farmers, including Jim and Jennifer Pike, owners of Pike Farms in Sagaponack. The well-known Pike farmstand is a tidy, impressive display of the just-picked bounty of the farm located behind it. In 2007, the Pikes were on the verge of selling their six-acre farm to a developer. But soon enough, they were powerfully buoyed by the entire community, who rallied to prevent the family farm from closing down. The Peconic Land Trust worked to raise money, as did Suffolk County, which now holds the long-term lease to the land. Today, the Pikes continue to farm, as their family has done for more than thirty years.

When planning his recipes, Jason says, "I find out what's going on from the farmers and make my menu decision from there. They let me know what's available and when." He prefers the farmers telling him what they have available rather than asking them to grow things for him.

Jason's wife, Almond Sun, whom he met in San Francisco and for whom his restaurants are named, is an avid gardener. She and Jason grow fruits, vegetables, and other produce at the local community-supported agriculture (CSA) organization, the Eco East End Co-op (EECO), as well as growing food at the restaurant.

Jason continues to learn by eating and by talking with other chefs in the tight Long Island restaurant community. Now, with two successful restaurants under their belts, Jason and Eric have opened up two more restaurants on Fire Island: the fine dining Blue Whale at Fire Island Pines and the grab-and-go Canteen, both of which feature ingredients from local sources.

Grilled Quail with a Warm Beet, Frisée, and Pistachio Salad

Serves 4

4 semiboneless quail (quail with all bones removed except the
  leg and wing bones)
3 tbsp. honey
2 tbsp. sherry vinegar
2 tbsp. grapeseed oil (canola would also be fine)
3 sprigs fresh sage
1 tsp. cracked black peppercorns
kosher salt, to taste
1 1/2 c. roasted baby beets, mixed colors, chopped to
  large dice
1 head frisée, cleaned (core and dark green leaves discarded)
3 tbsp. pistachios, roasted and shelled
5 chives, cut to matchstick size

About 5 hours before you plan to eat, lay the quail in 1 layer in a small casserole dish or Tupperware container. They should fit snugly. In a mixing bowl, combine the honey, vinegar, oil, sage, and peppercorns. Whisk vigorously for a moment. Pour the mixture over the quail. Cover with plastic wrap, and chill for about 5 hours.

Heat the grill. Remove the quail from the marinade (reserve the marinade), and season with salt. Put the quail on the hottest part of the grill. You want to crisp the skin before the quail gets overcooked in the middle. Quail is best when pink. If the grill is nice and hot, the bird shouldn't need to be on the grill for more than 2 1/2 to 3 minutes (2 minutes on one side, 30 to 60 seconds on the other).

While the quail is cooking, put the reserved marinade in a nonreactive saucepot and heat it on high heat. As soon as the marinade comes to a simmer, take it off the heat and pour it through a strainer to remove the sage and black pepper.

Put the beets, frisée, and nuts in a mixing bowl. Season with salt, and toss. Add the warm marinade. (You may not need it all.) Toss again. Divide the salad between four warm salad plates.

When you take the quail off the grill, let them rest for a moment, then cut each in half. Crisscross the halves on top of the salads. Garnish with the chives, and serve.

English Pea and Mint Soup with a Parmesan Flan and Smoked Bacon

Serves 6

SOUP BASE:

2 tbsp. butter

4 large leeks, white part only, split in half and thoroughly rinsed (they can be sandy)

1 large russet potato, peeled and diced medium

salt, to taste

1/2 c. dry white wine

1 sprig each fresh thyme, parsley, and tarragon

1 bay leaf

1 rib celery, diced

1 qt. chicken stock (if using a store-bought product, dilute with half water)

1/4 c. crème fraîche

salt and white pepper, to taste

In a heavy-bottomed pot on a low flame, put the butter, leeks, potato, diced celery, and a couple pinches of salt. Stir often with a wooden spoon until the potatoes and leeks become translucent. You don't want the vegetables to take on any color, so pay attention and maintain a low flame. Add the wine. Tie up the herbs and bay leaf in a bundle with butcher's twine, and add the bunch to the pot. When the wine is no longer releasing an alcohol aroma, add the stock.

Simmer until the potatoes are soft (approximately 20 minutes). Take the herbs out of the pot. Purée the mixture in a blender with the crème fraîche. Adjust the seasoning with salt and pepper. Sometimes the soup needs a squeeze of lemon as well.

PEA PURÉE:

2 c. shelled English peas

2 nice handfuls baby spinach

salt, to taste

Blanch the peas in a pot of heavily salted water until they are tender. Immediately transfer them to a blender. Quickly blanch the spinach in the same water. Add it to the blender. Purée the spinach and peas with about a cup of the soup base. Cool immediately to maintain the vibrant color.

FLAN:

1 c. heavy cream

1/3 c. grated Parmesan

2 egg yolks

salt and white pepper

cooking spray

Preheat oven to 350 degrees. In a saucepot, bring the cream to a simmer. Whisk in the cheese, and let the mixture reduce slightly.

Put the yolks in a mixing bowl. Slowly whisk the cream into the yolks. Adjust the seasoning with salt and pepper.

Coat six 2-oz. ramekins or shot glasses with cooking spray. Divide the flan mixture among the molds. Put the flans in a hot-water bath, cover it with several layers of plastic wrap, and put it in the oven on the middle shelf. Cook until the flans are set up—about a half hour.

ASSEMBLY:

1/4 c. bacon lardons

1/4 c. homemade croutons

1 tbsp. mint, chiffonade

Divide the mint, bacon, and croutons into six warm soup bowls. In the center of each bowl, place one flan. In a saucepot, warm the soup base. Whisk in the pea purée. Either put the bowls on the table as they are and serve the soup tableside, or divide the soup into bowls and serve.

Foody's

Chef Bryan Futerman
Hayground School Children's Garden

The extended family of third-generation cook Chef Bryan Futerman owned and ran four delicatessens at one point, in addition to a catering business, and as the oldest of three children, Bryan was always an eager cook in their businesses. The only real question was what *kind* of cook he could be.

His mother was a great influence. "She opened my eyes to so much. She'd take me to the city's great restaurants including the Russian Tea Room, Zabar's, and Dino de Laurentis DDL Food Show gourmet shop," he recalls.

Bryan grew up in the Dix Hills area of Long Island in the 1970s. In the mid 1980s, he attended Denver University's School of Hotel and Restaurant Management where he had fun cooking for his fraternity family. In recognition of his food obsession—and with a nod to his surname—they bestowed upon him the nickname "Foody." The shoe fit.

After graduation, he returned to New York to work with his father as manager of the family's Woodbury Kosher Gourmet Deli for five years. But he knew he wanted to do other, more creative culinary explorations. In 1993, he took night classes at Peter Kump's cooking school, the Institute of Culinary Education (ICE), while working in the family catering business by day. When it came time for Bryan's externship, his instructor, Ann Altermann, recommended Westmoreland Bistro, James Beard Award–winner Chef Caprial Pence's restaurant, outside Portland, Oregon.

After a year, Bryan was offered an opportunity to be the executive chef at a huge ski-resort restaurant in Lincoln, New Hampshire. He quickly instituted a menu of good, local cuisine updated in a fresh style, which helped turn the resort into a success. In 1994, he and his wife, Jennifer, got married and decided to move back to Long Island to be nearer to the Futerman family. Bryan got a job working for Chef Guy Reuge, owner of Mirabelle, and worked his way up first to sous chef then to chef de cuisine. When it was time for Bryan to spread his wings, Reuge helped him garner a position at Café Boulud in New York City.

Culinary school had taught him technique and how to tap into his creativity, but Michelin-starred Andrew Carmellini and his team taught him the *art* of cooking. Carmellini insisted on local products and farm-fresh food and embraced a variety of tastes and ingredients.

Though he was learning a lot, Bryan was commuting six days a week to work in a physically demanding kitchen environment alongside a lot of younger guys. So when Guy Reuge called and asked him to come back to Mirabelle as chef de cuisine, he jumped at the chance.

"I learned a lot from Guy—he's the consummate French chef," says Bryan. "He was so resourceful and creative. He respected the food too. He never stepped in front of the ingredients." Together, Bryan and Guy visited the Long Island farmstands, picked up local oysters and every fish species found on the island from the area's fishermen, and accepted every kind of bird the hunters would bring in.

In April 2001, Bryan landed another great job working for Chef Joe Realmuto at the world-famous Nick & Toni's. It was here Bryan first realized the scope and vast creative and community-enhancing opportunities the Slow Food movement offered. Bryan began to understand what "slow food" meant to him: taking delicious, locally grown vegetables and roasting them in the restaurant's famous wood oven.

After helping open and teach cooking classes at La Fondita, a family-style Italian salumeria, Bryan says he realized he "needed to do his own thing," so he opened Foody's in Water Mill. It is a modest restaurant that offers delicious, sustainable, healthy comfort food.

"My wife and I asked ourselves, 'Here we are in the middle of the most beautiful countryside: farms and beaches, so what do people want to eat?'" Bryan recalls. The answer shouted out to them from the yawning mouths of the wide-open oven doors: *pizza*.

Bryan invested in a custom wood-burning grill and promptly made arrangements to bring in locally harvested cherry-wood logs, which today perfume the surrounding area with a subtle cherry fragrance. He also developed a natural, homemade pizza dough using Long Island honey, atop which he builds nothing-like-it pizzas with only local toppings, from cheeses to tomatoes to vegetables.

"There is a little bit of the Hamptons in every slice," he proclaim

Together with Chef Joe Realmuto, Bryan developed Springs Seedlings, an edible-schoolyard project in Springs, Long Island. The program was inspired by Hayground School, a four-season after-school program managed by master gardener Jon Snow that includes raised-bed gardens, chickens, and a culinary center where the children cook every day with produce picked straight from the gardens. Every Friday, the children host a farmstand at the weekly farmers' market that takes place on a corner of the Hayground School in Bridgehampton. Local chefs take turns teaching the children how to cook what they harvest, how to clean fish, and how to compost.

With Foody's, Bryan has worked hard to establish a "sense of place" for the local citizens and tourists alike by celebrating the home-grown bounty of Long Island. Regardless of where his path may take him, Bryan aims to improve the community by combining his three passions—education, gardening, and cooking.

Pizza with Local Fresh Vegetables

Pizza with Local Fresh Vegetables

One 12-inch pizza serves 2; one 16-inch pizza serves 4

PIZZA DOUGH:

6 1/2 lb. high-gluten flour (such as All Trumps brand)
3/4 c. kosher salt (such as Diamond Crystal brand)
2 qt. water
1/4 c. extra virgin olive oil
2 tbsp. local honey
1 oz. fresh yeast
vegetable oil, for the proofing pans

Combine the flour and salt in the bowl of a stand-up mixer with a dough hook. In a separate container, combine the water, oil, and honey. Sprinkle in the yeast. Stir with a whisk to combine well.

Add the wet ingredients to the mixer bowl, and turn mixer on low speed. Be sure all of the ingredients combine well. Use a rubber spatula to scrape the sides after a minute or two to get the dry and wet ingredients together, then let the machine knead the dough for 15 minutes. When the dough is ready, it should be smooth, elastic, and slightly sticky.

Remove the dough from the bowl to a worktable. Cut it into pieces, and scale it out for individual pizzas: 20 oz. for a 16- to 18-inch pizza, 10 oz. for a 12-inch pizza, 5 oz. for a 10-inch pizza. Shape the dough into balls and put into oiled pans with lids. Allow them to rest in the refrigerator overnight. This recipe yields seventeen 10-oz. dough balls or eight to nine 20-oz. dough balls.

PIZZA:

extra flour
pizza sauce
fresh mozzarella, sliced
fresh local vegetables: spinach, tomato, garlic
local vegetables, diced and grilled: eggplant, zucchini, yellow squash, peppers, onions, carrots, chili peppers, broccoli rabe, wild mushrooms
basil, chiffonade

Preheat the oven to 550 degrees to 600 degrees. Gently remove a ball of dough from its pan, keeping its round shape, and place it into a bowl with some flour. Coat it with a dusting of flour. Remember that the bottom of the dough ball will become the top of the pizza. Use your fingers to pinch the outside edge of the dough ball, allowing the edge to form the outside crust, almost like a rope moving through your hands, all the way around the circumference of the pizza pan. Then press out the dough on the worktable; stretch the dough, keeping it round, and continue stretching until the dough is thin and the correct size.

Move the pizza crust, bottom up, onto a floured pizza peel, and use a ladle to spread a coating of pizza sauce evenly onto the crust. Place slices of cheese on top of the sauce. Add your selection of vegetables, sprinkling them evenly over the pizza. Garnish with torn basil leaves.

Gently slide the pizza onto a pizza stone or directly into the oven. Bake until the bottom is evenly brown and crisp and the cheese shows a slight browning. Remove the pizza from the oven with the pizza peel. Cut and serve immediately.

Cherry Wood–Smoked Brisket

Serves 8–10

1 c. kosher salt
1 c. ground black pepper
1 c. granulated garlic
1 c. Hungarian paprika
fresh whole brisket (approximately 8 lb.)
2 large Spanish onions, sliced

Combine salt, pepper, garlic, and paprika in a bowl to create a spice rub. Liberally season the fresh brisket with the spice rub mixture, completely coating the meat, top and bottom, with a heavy coating of spices. Allow it to marinate in the refrigerator, covered with plastic wrap, for 24 hours.

Remove the brisket from the refrigerator. Reseason the meat evenly with the spice rub, and place it on a metal rack. Heat a barbecue grill or smoker. Place the brisket and a metal rack over a sheet tray with a water bath. Smoke, fully covered, at a moderate temperature over a smoldering cherry-wood fire for 4 to 8 hours. Add water to the bath periodically through the smoking process.

Preheat the oven to 450 degrees. Remove the brisket from the rack, and transfer it to a heavy roasting pan. Add the sliced onions and the liquid remaining in the water bath. Add enough fresh water so there is about 1/2 inch in the roasting pan. Cover the pan tightly with aluminum foil, and braise the meat in oven for 1 1/2 to 2 1/2 hours, until a fork inserted in all points of the meat offers little resistance and the meat is tender.

Transfer the brisket from the roasting pan to a platter. Strain and degrease the braising liquid to make a natural juice for the brisket. Adjust the seasoning with some of the spice rub mixture. Slice the brisket with a sharp slicer across the grain, and trim of visible fat as you go. Serve hot with natural juice and with barbecue sauce on the side.

Watermelon–Red Pepper Gazpacho

Serves 10

1 c. white wine

3 red peppers, cleaned of seeds and cut in large pieces

1 sweet onion (such as Vidalia or Walla Walla), peeled and sliced

salt and pepper, to taste

1 seedless watermelon

juice of 2 lemons

1 jalapeño pepper, cleaned of seeds and diced

hot sauce, to taste

1 red onion, finely diced (brunoise, or 1/8-inch cubes)

1/2 bunch celery, finely diced (brunoise, or 1/8-inch cubes)

In a heavy-bottomed pot with a tight-fitting lid, add the white wine, red peppers, and sweet onion. Add salt and pepper to taste. Bring the white wine to a boil over high heat, then turn down to low. Allow the vegetables to steam for approximately 20 minutes. The red pepper and onion should be very soft. Do not allow the cooking liquid to dry; add some water, if needed. Remove from the heat, and let cool in refrigerator.

Remove all of the flesh from the watermelon, and place it into a large, deep container. Add the cold red pepper mixture and any remaining liquid to the watermelon. Add lemon juice, jalapeño, salt, pepper, and a few dashes of hot sauce to taste.

Using an immersion blender on high speed, purée everything until liquefied. Strain the gazpacho through a fine-mesh China cap strainer. Stir in the red onion and celery. Adjust the seasoning to taste. Serve very cold and in chilled bowls or cups.

Southfork Kitchen

Chef Joe Isidori

Mecox Bay Dairy

For Joe Isidori, cooking was always a family affair. His grandmother's Italian restaurant, the Villa Nova, flourished for many years in New York City's Diamond district. This is where his father learned how to cook, eventually owning several successful restaurants. Joe's grandfather was a butcher; his uncles were chefs.

There was no escape. Cooking was Joe's destiny.

After Joe was born, the entire family—all three generations—moved from the Bronx to Westchester, close to Yonkers. You could say it was a food move. All that property was mere acreage to raise more produce, along with additional space to air-dry Italian sausages and store fresh-from-the-garden canned foodstuffs.

After school, Joe worked prep in the kitchen of his family's restaurants. He moved up to full-time cook at age seventeen. After high school, Joe attended art school in New York City, majoring in graphic design. At the same time, the siren song of the restaurant kitchen beckoned.

Joe was soon working in Manhattan on a revolving door schedule in some of the city's best high-end restaurants. For free. "I had to prove myself," Joe says. "I sensed they wouldn't hire some kid from Yonkers with an accent so I offered to work for free on a nightly basis until they could see I knew what I was doing."

He had no problem proving his mettle, but then it hit him: "*This is what I'm supposed to be doing.*"

He told his father he wanted to go to culinary school, but his father had always believed his son would pursue a more upwardly mobile career. He also believed that Joe surely had learned everything he needed to know about cooking growing up in the family business, and school cost money they didn't have.

So Joe got a scholarship. At a friend's suggestion, a reviewer for the school surreptitiously had dinner at the Isidoris' Italian restaurant and was sufficiently impressed to offer him a scholarship to the Culinary Institute of America (CIA), where he was soon wowing the instructors.

Displaying a keen instinct for just how far talent and technique could take a good cook, Joe chose to serve his externship with Chef Michael Schwartz at Nemo in South Beach, Florida. Joe returned as sous chef after graduation and then, four years later was appointed chef de cuisine. Ultimately, the duo earned a four-star review from restaurant critics in the *Miami Sun Sentinel*. As early as the late 1990s, Nemo was weaving only local produce into its dishes, and Joe learned to develop a network of farmers and suppliers.

Missing his family and New York, however, Joe eventually returned home, and after less than a year, the Trump Organization recruited him. As a relentlessly loyal employee for nearly six years, Joe served as corporate executive chef for Donald Trump's private resorts, doing whatever Trump needed, at any time. In total, Joe advised on eight different Trump properties.

"It was an unprecedented and unique learning experience. It made me who I am," Joe says.

From 2003 to 2005, Joe refurbished the sumptuous restaurant at the DeLorean golf course in New Jersey for Trump, earning his Michelin stars and the coveted Rising Star Award from StarChefs.com. In 2007, he opened the exclusive DJT restaurant in Las Vegas, where, to ensure delivery of the best ingredients, he established an enterprising system of mobile on-site chef "concierges" driving to Santa Monica to alert him to the day's best comestibles. Joe also exploited the University of Nevada–Las Vegas testing programs for stone fruit and honeybee hives.

It was all coming up aces until the economy crashed a year later and the DJT restaurant couldn't sustain the hand it was dealt. With the restaurant's shuttering and his newfound passion for sustainability, Joe was ready to move to the place he knew captured everything he wanted to pursue as his next culinary chapter: Long Island. When NYTimes.com food writer Bruce Buschel was searching for an executive chef for his soon-to-open sustainable seafood restaurant in 2010, he hired Joe to run Southfork Kitchen in the Hamptons, reportedly having never personally tasted his food.

Seasonal, local ingredients spark Joe's cooking creations, and he enhances his dishes with products from Art Ludlow's Mecox Bay Dairy.

Art grew up on the farm he currently runs, but it wasn't always a small family operation. For years, his father grew Long Island potatoes and operated East End Dairy, a commercial farm, but it wasn't long after Art took over that he became disillusioned with the prospect of shipping his entire crop off the island. With an extraordinary focus on the best quality and flavor, Art returned exclusively to dairy farming, producing five handcrafted cheeses. "I like to say I turned the clock back."

Mecox Bay Dairy now makes a high-end food that is unmatched in taste and nutrition and sells a little over half its cheese output to farmers' markets, with the remainder going to cheese shops and to chefs. About eighty percent is sold within thirty miles of Bridgehampton. "I believe it's important to give people, especially chefs, the time for food—to have that dialogue about food production," says Art.

Joe Isidori's cooking has been described as timeless, but his menu changes monthly, reflecting his commitment to seasonal, local food resources. This simple, pure approach that focuses attention on inherent, natural flavor has sustained populations—and generations. He grew up on it.

Korean-Style PEI Mussels with House-Made Kim Chi and Smoked Bacon

Serves 8–10

MUSSEL FUME (YIELD: 2 QT.):

 2 tbsp. lemongrass, chopped
 2 tbsp. ginger, chopped
 2 tbsp. garlic, chopped
 2 tbsp. shallot, minced
 4 c. rice wine (such as Sho Xing brand)
 4 c. clam juice
 8 each parsley stems and cilantro stems
 1 tbsp. whole black peppercorns
 2 tbsp. spice base (such as Kim Chi brand)
 4 pods star anise
 2 c. heavy cream

Sweat the lemongrass, garlic, ginger, and shallot (cook gently with a lid on low-medium to low heat). Add the rice wine, and reduce by half. Add the clam juice along with the parsley, cilantro, spices, and cream. Reduce slightly, strain, and reserve for plating.

KOREAN PEPPER SAUCE (YIELD: 3 C.):

 2 c. Korean red pepper purée
 1 tbsp. garlic, micro-planed
 1 tbsp. ginger, micro-planed
 1/2 c. fresh lime juice
 1/2 c. rice vinegar

Mix all ingredients until they are well combined. Reserve.

BASIL OIL (YIELD: 2 C.):

 2 c. Thai basil leaves, blanched
 1 tsp. powdered sugar
 2 c. grapeseed oil

Place all of the ingredients in a food processor, and blend on high until a bright green color is achieved. Strain the mixture through a linen-like napkin, and reserve.

HOUSE-MADE KIM CHI (YIELD: 2–3 QT.):

 10 Kirby pickles
 salt for seasoning
 2 carrots, shredded
 2 c. fish sauce
 1 c. shrimp, salted
 1 c. scallion, sliced
 1 c. garlic chives, sliced
 2 c. Korean hot pepper paste
 1/2 c. dried Korean pepper flake

 1 tbsp. sugar
 1/2 c. garlic, micro-planed
 1/2 c. ginger, micro-planed

Slice the pickles in half lengthwise. Season them with salt, and let stand for about an hour. Afterward, arrange the pickles in an airtight container with shredded carrot. Mix all of the remaining ingredients together, and pour over the Kirbys. Mix, then store in a dry pantry for up to 2 to 3 days. After that, store in the refrigerator.

Note: Pickles do not have to be stored in a dry place. They can go directly into the refrigerator. For each dish, chop up two pieces of Kirby Kim Chi and reserve.

MUSSELS:

 2 shallots, diced
 1/4 to 1/2 c. grapeseed oil
 15–20 mussels per person
 1 c. Mussel Fume
 salt and pepper, to taste
 2 tbsp. bacon lardoons, rendered
 2 c. napa cabbage, chiffonade

In a shallow pan, sweat some shallot in grapeseed oil (cook gently with a lid on low-medium to low heat). Add 15 to 20 mussels and 1 c. fume. Season with salt and pepper. Cook until open. Remove mussels and reserve hot. Add the rendered bacon lardoons and chiffonade of napa cabbage to the pan. Cook until the sauce is reduced slightly and the cabbage is tender.

PLATING:

 Korean Pepper Sauce
 Basil Oil
 1/2 c. breakfast radish, sliced
 1/2 c. Thai basil leaves
 1/2 c. cilantro leaves
 1/4 c. fried garlic chips
 1/4 c. fried shallots
 1/4 c. rendered bacon lardoons
 2 c. chiffonade napa cabbage

Place the mussels and cabbage in a noodle-style bowl and drizzle with Korean Pepper Sauce and Basil Oil. Garnish with Kim Chi, radish, Thai basil, cilantro, garlic chips, and shallots. Serve while very hot. Griddled Texas toast is a great accompaniment to this dish.

Note: Each serving consists of 15 to 20 mussels. The listed *mis en place* will be able to produce 8 to 10 servings.

Nonni's Ricotta Gnocchi
with Tomato and Basil

Serves 4

GNOCCHI DOUGH (YIELD: APPROXIMATELY 1 LB.):
- **1 1/2–2 c. all-purpose flour**
- **1 lb. fresh ricotta cheese**
- **1 c. pecorino cheese, grated**
- **touch of sea salt**
- **2 tbsp. extra virgin olive oil**
- **2 whole eggs**

Mix all of the dry ingredients slowly in a bowl, starting with the flour first, then adding the wet ingredients. Mix until the desired texture is achieved. Add or subtract flour according to the feel of the dough. Knead for about 10 minutes, and allow to rest in a bowl covered with a damp cloth for about an hour.

When the dough is ready, pull off small ball-like pieces and roll them into long snake-like shapes. Cut each into roughly 1-inch pieces. Roll in flour or semolina to prevent sticking, place on flat sheet pan, and freeze for about 1 to 2 hours or until firm/hard.

TOMATO AND BASIL SAUCE (YIELD: APPROXIMATELY 1 QT.):
- **1/4 c. extra virgin olive oil**
- **6 cloves garlic, sliced**
- **1/4 c. shallot, sliced**
- **pinch pepperoncini flakes**
- **1 qt. canned tomatoes (San Marzano style or home-canned garden variety)**
- **sea salt and black pepper, to taste**
- **1 c. garden basil leaves**

To a hot pan, add olive oil, garlic, and shallot. When the garlic has browned, add pepperoncini; after about 10 seconds, add the tomatoes and season. Cook for 3 to 5 minutes. Toss in fresh basil leaves, and reserve.

ASSEMBLY:
- **fresh grated pecorino cheese, to garnish**
- **basil, to garnish**
- **extra virgin olive oil, to garnish**

In a pot of boiling water, boil the gnocchi until tender. In a sauté pan, add a little of the tomato sauce and toss your cooked gnocchi with the sauce and a little of the pasta cooking water (very little). Coat the gnocchi completely, place it in a serving bowl, and spoon the desired amount of the remaining sauce over the gnocchi. Finish with a sprinkle of fresh grated pecorino cheese, more basil, and a drizzle of extra virgin olive oil.

Arctic Char with Miso, Grapefruit, and Yuzu

Serves 6–8

MISO GLAZE (YIELD: APPROXIMATELY 1 PT.):
- **1 c. organic white miso**
- **1 c. sake**
- **1/2 c. mirin**

Combine all until smooth, and reserve.

YUZU BUTTER SAUCE:
- **1/4 c. yuzu juice**
- **1/4 c. pink grapefruit juice**
- **1/4 c. verjus blanc**
- **1/4 c. mirin**
- **1/2 c. pink pickled ginger**
- **sea salt, to taste**
- **1 1/2 lb. butter**

Mix all of the ingredients together and reduce by half. Place the hot liquid in a food processor. Slowly blend and mount with the butter. When completely emulsified, keep in warm place until needed.

ASSEMBLY:
- **6–8 (7 oz.) Arctic char filets**
- **red grapefruit segments**
- **radish, sliced**
- **Asian greens (bok choy or other)**
- **chili oil**
- **sesame seeds, toasted**
- **scallions, chopped**
- **wild salmon roe (optional)**

Spread a layer of Miso Glaze on top of one 7 oz. portion of skinless Arctic char. Then broil the fish in the oven until it is cooked through slightly and the Miso Glaze is brown/caramelized on top. Spoon 1 to 2 oz. Yuzu Butter Sauce onto a plate. Garnish with red grapefruit segments, sliced radish, and any type of steamed or sautéed Asian greens (i.e., bok choy). Serve fish on top, and finish with a drizzle of chili oil, toasted sesame seeds, chopped scallion, and, if you want an extra bite, a teaspoon of wild salmon roe.

Arctic Char
with Miso, Grapefruit & Yuzu

1770 House

Chef Kevin Penner
Quail Hill Farm

Chef Kevin Penner can be forgiven for believing that food and cooking are natural extensions of agriculture. After all, Kevin grew up on a farm just outside Iowa City and lived the complete farm life experience.

Of German and Russian ancestry, he remembers eating at home with his family every night and on weekends with the extended family. Enjoying the bounty of the harvest and the hunt, Kevin also foraged for nature's more hidden treasures, including wild asparagus and berries. "We ate so many family specialty recipes fulfilled with local food," recalls Kevin.

While Kevin's father worked on the railroad, his grandparents and uncles farmed more than a thousand acres each with beans, corn, and livestock. In the summer, Kevin worked the farms along with the family, mastering horticulture and agriculture, tending the sheep, cattle, and pigs—and fulfilling every kid's fantasy of driving a tractor.

Kevin's first exposure to the professional culinary world came when he worked in restaurants to help pay for college tuition while attending the University of Iowa for a degree in philosophy. Kevin, however, viewed restaurants the way others might view a passport: cooking was his tasty ticket to the world, and he used it to travel. His launch into the world of professional cooking was as pastry chef in Seattle's world-class department store, Nordstrom, where for almost two years he strove to perfect his flaky, buttery, layered croissants and Danish. That detailed nuance, precision, and alchemy further ignited his decision to pursue a career in cooking.

He moved to Chicago in 1990 and helped open the award-winning Coco Pazzo restaurant.

"It was an invaluable experience," says Kevin. "I learned the complete process—from how to choose the ingredients to how to make the dish and how you plate it. Even the bread was baked to order," he adds. To Kevin, the experience confirmed freshness makes the best products.

A few years later, Kevin was discovered by Drew Nieporent, one of America's most respected and celebrated restaurateurs, at the annual Chicago Restaurant Show. Drew, a managing partner in the East Hampton restaurant Della Femina, scheduled to open in August, offered Kevin the job of executive chef. "I had always planned to work my way around the country and see different things," says Kevin. "I'd done the West and Midwest and this seemed like the next logical step."

The farmers, fishermen, and artisanal food makers in Long Island at that time were mostly entrepreneurial, but others had to be nudged along. In the early days of the field-to-table foray, Kevin played a key role in developing a direct connection to locals for fresher taste—and to minimize food transportation costs.

Kevin opted in early to "give credit where it's due" and put the food providers on the menu. Recipes start with in-season, local ingredients, and Quail Hill, the longest-running community-supported organic farm on Long Island, is an ideal source.

The bond between Kevin and Quail Hill's Scott Chaskey was sealed at the farm's annual family-style dinner event, At the Common Table, created to celebrate the family of artists and craftspeople who grow the food and those who prepare it.

"We are linked by our respect for the land and for the inherent possibilities found in nature: our local resources and the bounty of our farms," explains Scott. He readily acknowledges Kevin's extraordinary commitment and that of other East End chefs who contribute to Quail Hill and the Peconic Land Trust's ongoing farm activities, especially cooking for At the Common Table, served in the apple orchard.

While Kevin knows his crops, he rarely asks the farmers to grow things specifically for him, outside of heirloom tomatoes and some vegetables. "I pretty much take what they give me." He adds, "Most of the farmers here have great produce and a pretty good balance between their consumer and restaurant sales. The local chefs offer the farmers a higher purchase volume than their farmstands can, which in turn compensates for the difference in price," explains Kevin.

Kevin says it can be challenging to cook in winter. "The pickings can seem mighty slim," he jokes. He prefers to use fewer ingredients that are of the highest quality and work the season's best into a variety of dishes that are striking in culinary design and sumptuous pairings.

Kevin was recruited to help open the historic and charmingly elegant 1770 House in 2002—just in time for the summer splendids. The owners undertook a complete renovation of the inn and restaurant, increasing the size and changing the ambience to a more refined atmosphere where Kevin could emphasize greater quality and create a smaller, focused menu with seasonally driven changes, both for the 1770 House and the other two restaurants he runs for the management group: The Grill on Pantigo and Cittanuova. Kevin maintains his strong ties to local businesses, secures unique products, and simplifies the manipulation of the food. Having grown up on a farm and eaten fresh from the field, he is now part of the East End's culinary firmament—a true-to-his-roots, homegrown fixture.

Looking into the future, Kevin vows to keep it simple—to continue to put the best products on the plate. "People's lives are complex enough—they prefer a more casual dining experience. We strip away the pomp and pretense to achieve a dialed-down but deeper, more enduring food adventure."

Local Long Island Oysters
with Mignonette Sauce

Serves 4

One of the best locally "grown" foods on Long Island is the local oysters. When you top them with this mignonette made with locally grown shallots, it is a marriage made in heaven.

24 carefully scrubbed and well-chilled Fisher's Island oysters

MIGNONETTE:
**1 c. champagne vinegar
3 shallots from the garden, peeled, washed, and finely minced
1 tbsp. whole black peppercorns, crushed very coarsely with
  the back of a small sauté pan
platter covered in crushed ice**

Combine the vinegar, shallots, and peppercorns. Do this 1 day ahead of time, and store chilled.

To serve: Shuck each oyster, making sure to keep the oyster in the bottom (deeper) shell, and nestle them in the ice on the platter. Place the Mignonette (you won't need all of it) in a small ramekin, and put it on the platter with the oysters. Provide a couple of small demitasse spoons for the sauce as well. Spoon a little Mignonette onto each oyster, and slip one into your mouth. Cold, briney deliciousness!

Local Tomatoes
with Mozzarella di Bufala

Serves 4

Another favorite locally grown food from Long Island is the tomatoes we get in the summer. They are at their best in late August as a rule but sometimes earlier. One of my favorite ways to serve them is simply sliced with some mozzarella di bufala from Campania in Italy. All of it—a few small leaves of basil from the garden, a few drops of lemon juice, a little fruity olive oil from Liguria in Italy, and some coarse sea salt like that from Maldon—needs to be at room temperature.

4 medium-sized tomatoes, never having been chilled, washed and thickly sliced (I like just about any variety)

4 balls of mozzarella di bufala, bocconcini-size

12 very small basil leaves

1 tbsp. freshly squeezed lemon juice

4 tbsp. fruity olive oil (I prefer mine from Liguria, preferably pressed from taggiasca olives)

large pinch sea salt

Place the tomato slices on four small plates. Slice each ball of cheese in half, and place the tomatoes on top. Sprinkle with the basil leaves. Drizzle the lemon juice and olive oil evenly over each, and sprinkle with the sea salt.

Local Tuna Crudo

Serves 4

In August our local waters are brimming with fish of all sorts. Tuna is always nice. I like to serve it raw in the style of "crudo."

4 (4 oz.) pieces raw, trimmed tuna, thinly sliced

4 pinches Maldon sea salt

1 large shallot from the garden, finely minced

2 small radishes from the garden, minced

4 tsp. blood orange vinegar

4 tbsp. Ligurian olive oil

2 tbsp. chives from the garden, very thinly sliced

On each of four small plates, fan the tuna out into overlapping slices. Sprinkle each portion with the sea salt, shallots, and radishes. Next, sprinkle each portion with the blood orange vinegar and then the olive oil. Top each with the chives.

Fresno

Chef Gretchen Menser
Babinski Farm Stand

Born in Bolivia to American artists intent on pursuing a bohemian life-style, Chef Gretchen Menser grew up in exotic locales from Bali to Kuala Lumpur, Ibiza, and Germany. Her culinary awakening occurred in situ as she experienced the world's culture through its food and gardens.

Her hippie parents' home dining style gravitated more toward family in the larger, community sense. Everybody brought a favorite home-cooked dish. Ex pats or locals—all enjoyed the cultural cuisine of the country they were living in. Looking back, Gretchen says she loved her global gourmandizing, her garden experiences, and all the different flavors and savory imprints.

Following in her parents' fine art path after her college graduation, Gretchen worked in a New York City gallery specializing in antique floor coverings. But she was dismayed with interior designers guiding their clients to buy art and antiquities based on color swatches rather than provenance or beauty. When Gretchen visited a friend who was attending the Culinary Institute of America (CIA), she was more than intrigued and eventually gained acceptance to the school.

Gretchen remarks that at the age of twenty-three she was an "older" student, and not many were women either. This one-two punch might have been daunting for fainter hearts. "It's physical work to be sure but the CIA pushed me to be ever more determined to succeed." She graduated top of her class.

In 1993, she began a short-lived externship at the Park Avenue Café, completing that part of the program at Nick & Toni's restaurant in East Hampton. Her parents were now living in Quogue in the Hamptons, and she was immediately smitten with the South Fork upon visiting them. The fresh from the garden cooking experience at Nick & Toni's was so profound Gretchen returned to work at Nick & Toni's after graduation, where she spent the first three years of her culinary career at the salad station. She picked fresh vegetables and herbs in the garden and bought fish at the back door from local fishermen.

In late 1996 when the owners of Nick & Toni's set out to open another restaurant, Rowdy Hall, Gretchen was asked to be the executive chef. From the start, she continued to nurture her own culinary style with her hand firmly on the budget control button.

Her early success was based in part on consistent experimentation with sublime local ingredients to creatively make the food interesting and memorable. With this new venture, it was her turn to develop her own relationships with local food artisans. She plumbed the back roads for farm-fresh goodies. "I'd often stop off for tomatoes at Bistrian Farms, who had a roadside stand during season," she says. "And when I couldn't take away any more, I'd say 'I'll be back later for a bushel of corn.'"

Gretchen held the helm at Rowdy Hall for three years. Subsequently, she was recruited to serve in various chef positions at a number of different restaurants that all opened to great promise but

became undone soon enough. At Fresno restaurant, she was brought in as executive chef to change things. The owners, Michael Nolan and David Lowenberg, wanted creativity. "They wanted me to take the food from where it was to a place with much more progressive menu offerings," she explains. Knowing the eyes eat first, she added bright and colorful "art" to Fresno's dishes, jazzing the guests with her graphic renderings before their first bite.

Fresh food has always been a priority for Gretchen. At Fresno, she and her chefs are fundamentally devoted to using fresh, local foodstuffs. "It's what drives the people who cook here," she says.

She and the owners are building a garden surrounding Fresno's patio. Gretchen also sources from local farms and greenmarkets. She helplessly confesses to loving tomatoes too much. "From Babinski Farm Stand, Mike Babinski brings me the most beautiful tomatoes—almost too beautiful to touch," she says wistfully.

Mike grew up on his family's farm in the Hamptons, and today, he and his sister farm just down the road in Water Mill. The growing season kicks off at the end of June, at which time more than a thousand plants are tucked into the rich black gold that is Long Island growing soil. Mike says they can get two to three harvests a year, with planting seasons that feature heirloom tomatoes like Brandywine, Farmette, and Beefsteak.

Chef and farmer were introduced through a mutual link on the East End food network, and when Mike first brought Gretchen a variety of what he grows, she carefully reviewed, admired, and sampled the firm yet juicy, distinctly nuanced, fresh-from-the-heat-of-the-farm treasures. She was seduced, and she and Mike have been food partners ever since. There is an enduring, honest pride in what Mike and his family do on the farm, and it shows.

Seasons drive menus, and, Gretchen says, "Fresno's customers—particularly the locals, along with year-round residents—want to know where their food comes from." She instructs the wait staff about the significant names on the menu that, in turn, narrate the food story for the guests about oysters from Greenport and striped bass from Montauk. Gretchen's kaleidoscope of homegrown recipes is shot through with tempting, new, never-tried-before flavors. At the same time, she believes her best food is memorable for its consistency and quality and for the fact that she is true to herself.

Braised Beef Short Ribs with Creamy Polenta and Halsey Farm Apple Gremolata

Serves 4

4 boneless beef short ribs

kosher salt and ground black pepper, to taste

2 tbsp. canola oil

1 (750 ml.) bottle of good red wine

1 (29 oz.) can tomato purée

2 ribs celery, diced medium

2 carrots, peeled and diced medium

3 small Spanish onions, peeled and diced medium

4 cinnamon sticks

4 tbsp. whole coriander seeds

4 tbsp. whole black peppercorns

4 whole star anise

5 sprigs rosemary

polenta, to serve

Preheat the oven to 300 degrees. Season the short ribs with kosher salt and ground black pepper. Sear the short ribs in a hot sauté pan with canola oil, and then transfer them to a large roasting pan. Set the roasting pan over the stove burners on medium heat, and add the red wine. Add the tomato purée, and bring up to a medium simmer. Add the diced *mire poix* (the celery, carrots, and onions) and all of the spices. Cover the pan with aluminum foil, and place it in the oven. Cook for 3 to 3 1/2 hours or until tender.

Remove the short ribs from the braising liquid and strain out all the vegetables and spices. Reduce the braising liquid by half.

For braising liquid: Place the liquid in a heavy-bottom stockpot, and bring it to a boil. Reduce to a simmer, and cook until half the amount remains. Portion the short ribs into 4 equal portions, and reheat them in the reduced braising liquid. Place each portion of short ribs over creamy polenta, sauce each rib with reduced braising liquid, and top with the Halsey Farm Apple Gremolata.

HALSEY FARM APPLE GREMOLATA:

2 medium apples

1 tbsp. freshly grated horseradish

zest of 1 each lemon, lime, and orange

1 tbsp. finely chopped Italian parsley

extra virgin olive oil

fresh lemon juice

kosher salt and ground black pepper, to taste

Use any apple you prefer. (If you can find local apples, use them.) On a Japanese mandolin fitted with the small teeth, finely grate the apples. Wash and peel the horseradish. Chop into small pieces, and place in a food processor until finely grated. In a bowl toss the apples with the horseradish, zest, and parsley, and drizzle with extra virgin olive oil and lemon juice. Season with kosher salt and ground black pepper to taste.

Crudo of Local Fluke

Serves 4

1/2–1 lb. sushi-grade fluke filet, skin off
1/2 seedless hot house cucumber
2 large radishes (red, French breakfast, or Easter egg)
1 large jalapeño, seeded, ribs removed and finely diced
4 tbsp. Ginger Oil (recipe to follow)
2 tbsp. fresh lime juice
Hawaiian pink sea salt, to taste

On the bias, thinly slice the fluke into approximately 1/2-oz. slices. Place the fluke on a plate overlapping the slices, 4 to 6 slices per plate. Use a Japanese mandolin to shave the cucumber and the radishes finely.

In a bowl, toss the cucumber, radishes, and jalapeño with the Ginger Oil and the lime juice. Place the salad on top of the sliced fluke, then drizzle the remaining Ginger Oil and lime juice over the fluke. Season with Hawaiian pink sea salt, to taste.

GINGER OIL:
1 lb. fresh ginger root
6 c. canola oil

Wash and rough chop the ginger (no need to remove the skin). Place the ginger and the oil in a large sauce pot, and bring to a boil. Reduce to a simmer, and cook for 3 hours. Transfer the ginger with the oil to a stainless steel bowl. Refrigerate until completely cooled. Strain the pieces of ginger out of the oil. Store the oil in a glass jar in the refrigerator.

Note: Ginger oil can be made days in advance and kept in the refrigerator for up to 1 month.

Chilled Babinski Heirloom **Tomato Soup** with Spicy Guacamole

Serves 4

6 lb. large local heirloom tomatoes (if you don't have local
  tomatoes, use the ripest ones you can find)
12 tbsp. extra virgin olive oil
kosher salt and ground black pepper, to taste

Wash the tomatoes, roughly chop. In batches, place 1 oz. olive oil and add the tomatoes to fill a blender three-quarters of the way to the top. Purée the tomatoes on high, and season with kosher salt and ground pepper to taste. Strain the puréed tomatoes through a fine-meshed sieve. Chill the soup completely. When cold, transfer the soup into four bowls and garnish with 1 tbsp. guacamole.

SPICY GUACAMOLE:
3 large ripe Haas avocados
1 large jalapeño
1 medium red onion
3 tbsp. chopped fresh cilantro
fresh lime juice, to taste
kosher salt, to taste

Slice and remove the seed of each avocado, remove the flesh, and roughly chop. Wash, remove the seeds and ribs of the jalapeño, and finely dice. Peel the red onion and finely dice. Place the avocados, jalapeño, and onion in a stainless steel bowl; add the cilantro. With a potato masher, mash the avocados until just slightly lumpy. Add fresh lime juice and salt to taste.

Note: Guacamole can be made 1 hour in advance. Lay plastic wrap directly on the guacamole, and store in the refrigerator.

The Living Room
at the Maidstone Inn

Chef James Carpenter
Open Minded Organics

Nothing in James Carpenter's early life prepared him for his stellar career as master chef at top-tier restaurants from Atlanta to Chicago to Long Island. Nothing except disciplined hard work and innate talent.

The circumspect James grew up in New York's Westchester County in a standard-issue suburban household. Meals weren't fancy, and with both parents working, he was required to help start dinners. Toiling in the family garden instilled in James an enduring respect for homegrown food. Working summers in local restaurants part-time opened the door of opportunity for a culinary career.

Immediately following high school graduation, James joined the U.S. Navy as, what else, a cook. James served on the USS *Midway*, stationed in Japan, where he was afforded the opportunity to enjoy the Far East and eat his way through the cultural cuisines of Hong Kong, the Philippines, and Thailand—an exotic and delicious counterpoint to his white bread, Betty Crocker childhood food experience.

After his honorable discharge from the Navy, James moved to Minneapolis for love. Professionally, he worked as a sous chef at the Hyatt Hotel for a few years before enrolling in the express program at Johnston & Wales culinary school in Charleston, South Carolina. Upon earning his diploma, he returned to Minneapolis to work at the flagship department store Dayton Hudson in the dining room kitchen. For five years, he prepared interpretive French cuisine for the dining room meals, as well as the retailer's food courts. He enjoyed the high-volume work and corporate structure at Dayton's, not unlike the military world he had known before.

In late 1997, when a culinary school friend, Sean Dody, asked him to take the helm at the Ritz-Carlton in Buckhead, Georgia, James discovered the lure of fine dining and never looked back. After a year, he moved to New Orleans where he learned Southern-style cooking with Susan Spicer at the restaurant Bayona in the French Quarter and as executive chef at Café Sbisa. In Charleston he learned a lot about Low Country cuisine and the emerging Slow Food initiative from a chef he refers to as the "godfather" of both: Chef Louis Osteen "was doing organic farm-to-table more than twenty years ago," claims James.

While James had grown up with a big family garden, it wasn't until Charleston and Atlanta that his thumb got truly green. At the Ritz-Carlton, he learned horticulture and gardening from his hero chef, Gunther Seeger, who taught him to seek out small farmers who would grow things specifically for the restaurant. Subsequently, the restaurant's impact on the local agricultural community and the quality and integrity of the food at the restaurant became fundamental components of James' culinary principles.

It's not a stretch then to learn that it was a *Southern*-style restaurant, Savannas, opening in *South*hampton, that brought James to Long Island.

When James arrived in the Hamptons in the late 1990s, he was delighted to see so many farms and the water teaming with seafood. Not unlike those Low Country forays, James visited the local farms, picking up produce at the myriad farmstands that punctuate the back roads. Today, the garden at the Maidstone is tenderly nurtured by James and his staff, growing herbs, vegetables, and fruits. James also works to discover and establish his network of local farms, including Open Minded Organics.

After attending a seminar in 2003, "It hit me. That's what I want to do," recollects Open Minded Organics' David Falkowski. And just like that, he was mushrooming. In fact, he started by building a laboratory in his attic and growing mushrooms in his backyard. After some initial success, he expanded his crop, moving the fungi to a larger grow house he built on family land.

While David comes from a family of Bridgehampton growers—his father ran a tree nursery on their fifteen acres of preserved farmland—he is the first to grow mushrooms. He developed an organic, sustainable mushroom farm and can boast of the extraordinary taste that is a result of the local soil and climate. David insists his mushrooms offer a seasonal, high-quality product to tempt foodies of all ilk. "Every year, the taste is a little different," he says, making the mushroom a particularly exciting muse for the chefs, especially as interpreted by James.

James changes the menu every couple of months based on homegrown seasonal availability, paired with everyday, tasty, kick-start additions, while keeping the iconic dishes his customers long for. The James Beard Foundation has invited James multiple times to cook his indulgent dinners for their prestigious American series.

He is proud to highlight the names of his American farmers and local food artisans on the Living Room's menu. It adds to the distinctive dining experience to share the narrative of where the food comes from, according to James. And it's a way to honor the food producers and convey James' respect for the process.

James sees the interest in local food continuing because he recognizes that people are more educated about food and where it comes from. "They want a simply prepared food story. It tastes better and is good for you." He adds, "Now more than ever we know we should eat within our zip code."

Rakmacka

Serves 4

A very Swedish open-face sandwich popular in the summer.

4 tbsp. Lemon Aioli
4 pieces crusty bread, sliced about 6 inches long
8 bibb lettuce leaves
1 vine-ripe Beefsteak tomato (try for 8 slices)
20 slices cucumber
2 hard-cooked organic eggs, cut into quarters
8 oz. Maine baby shrimp
1 avocado, ripe, cut into quarters, then sliced
black pepper and sea salt
olive oil

Spread the aioli on the bread slices, and then place avocado slices on the bread. Place the lettuce, tomato, cucumber, and egg wedges on the sandwich, and top that with the baby shrimp. You can give it a twist of black pepper and a pinch of sexy sea salt. A drizzle of good olive oil would be a nice finish. If you don't like shrimp, this recipe works well with jumbo lump crab meat or a good-quality tuna. Serve with salad on the side or in a big bowl to go family style.

LEMON AIOLI:
4 egg yolks
1 tsp. Dijon mustard
zest and juice of 1 lemon
pinch of sea salt
1 c. olive oil

Place all of the ingredients except the oil in a food processor. Turn on the food processor, and slowly drizzle in the olive oil. Store in a covered container in the refrigerator until ready to use.

Satur Farm Organic Green Salad

Serves 4

1 c. organic baby lettuce (a nice mixture)
4 or 5 organic radishes (multicolor, such as Easter egg or
   French breakfast), sliced thin
1 small bulb fennel, thinly shaved
1/4 c. mixed herbs (such as dill, parsley, tarragon, chervil,
   and chives)
4 tbsp. Merlot Red Wine Vinaigrette
fresh black pepper and sea salt

Toss all of the ingredients except the salt and pepper in a bowl.
Place a sophisticated pile in the center of four plates. Season with a
twist of fresh black pepper and a pinch of sea salt.

This is our basic green salad. Gussy it up with heirloom cherry tomatoes or slices of lemon cucumber. Whatever looks great at your
local farmstand is the right ingredient.

MERLOT RED WINE VINAIGRETTE:
   1/2 c. merlot vinegar
   1/4 c. shallots, finely diced
   1 clove garlic, minced
   1 c. extra virgin olive oil

Mix vinegar, shallots, and garlic. Let sit 15 minutes, then whisk in
oil slowly.

Toast Sgaken

Serves 4

8 oz. Maine baby shrimp
1/4 c. shallots, finely diced
2 tbsp. dill, chopped fine
extra virgin olive oil for drizzling, as needed
4 tbsp. crème fraîche
1/4 c. cucumber pickles, diced small
4 tbsp. caviar, fresh
1/2 c. very baby greens, or some herb salad
black pepper and sea salt, to taste
4 brioche slices, toasted and cut into triangles

Mix the shrimp with the shallot, dill, and a drizzle of oil. Line up
the plates, and place 4 tbsp. of the shrimp mixture, 1 tbsp. crème
fraîche, 1 spoonful of cucumber pickles, a dollop of caviar, and a
nice pinch of greens or herb salad. Drizzle with as much olive oil as
you like. Add a twist of black pepper and pinch of sea salt to finish.
Place toast points on the side.

Starr Boggs

Chef Starr Boggs
Starr Boggs Garden

If there existed a Culinary Walk of Fame (and why is there not one?), Chef Starr Boggs would have earned his star on it decades ago. Never mind the sparkling name association; his slow, soft-spoken, Gregory Peck style reveals a combination of confidence and humility that is two parts Southern gentlemen and two parts naturalist.

Starr has been involved with homegrown food since growing up on a farm on the eastern shore of Virginia, an area not unlike Long Island.

"Everything we ate we raised or fished for," he says. "We got seafood, including clams, crabs, rockfish, and oysters. We had dairy cows, chickens, hogs. Every year we had a hog killing and made sausage and scrapple."

Early in his youth, the members of his family were truck farmers; later they became custom farmers, supplying local canneries and granaries. Whatever they didn't raise on the farm, they grew in the garden. Every day, Starr worked outside in the garden and on the farm, harvesting the crops and working shoulder-to-shoulder with his father, grandfather, and the migrant laborers.

The family's kitchen was just as big a part of the farm as the garden and the fields, and Starr spent as much time there, with his mother and grandmother, as he did out on the farm. They canned and put up food for the winter, and he learned to cook—especially big dinners, which his family prepared for Sundays and holidays.

While attending the College of William and Mary, he started going out to fine-dining restaurants. Intrigued by the restaurants and needing the money, he started working as a kitchen apprentice in Colonial Williamsburg, and thus began his lifelong love affair with cooking.

Leaving college, he moved to Palm Beach, Florida, and there worked with a variety of French and Italian chefs. This in-the-kitchen experience served as his formal culinary training; he learned cooking techniques and the business of running a restaurant. He soon relocated north to Nantucket and started cooking with Chef Frank Lucas.

Shortly thereafter, a friend told him that someone he knew in Long Island needed a chef. Though Starr had never been to New York, he applied for the job at the Inn at Quogue and got it. He was immediately bewitched by the area and found his culinary oeuvre. In 1983, after only a few years on the job, he earned the restaurant its first *New York Times* review—and a great one too. Having made his mark, he opened his own restaurant in 1986—the first of four restaurants he's owned and managed over the course of his thirty-plus years of cooking on Long Island.

One of his first challenges when he came to the Inn at Quogue was finding local food resources. The mentality at that time dictated that getting tomatoes meant ordering a box from a produce-delivery guy. Starr instead began driving the back roads, searching for farms and farmstands to provide him with that night's dinner ingredients. In later years, he introduced his young apprentices to "shopping the

market," sending them careening around dirt roads to his farming partners to fulfill the daily menu's shopping list. Starr was able to build a network of food producers quickly, in part, because of his clear respect for the land and those who work it.

"I was a farmer, and I know what it's like to work the land—the difficulties and the problems. So in talking to the farmer, I would never ask for something out of season," he explains. "I think the farmers respected that. . . . I appreciated their hard work and could sense their pride that I was using local ingredients."

In the course of building his food network, Starr beseeched farmers to sell to him directly. He and the farmers made up their business relationship as they went along, creating an expanded market for the farmers and a food infrastructure at the same time.

Starr's lifelong dedication to gardens and farms infuses his imaginative recipes. "I learned early on to get creative if an ingredient hadn't ripened in time to fulfill a menu recipe," he says. He works with the subtleties of what food is available and challenges himself to produce delicious, memorable dishes.

In the restaurant's rooftop garden, perched over the kitchen, Starr and Chef Frank Lucas grow more than twenty potted fresh vegetables and herbs, including cherry tomatoes, bay laurel, and sage. They research heirloom seed catalogs in the winter and start the plants indoors before moving them out in the spring. Diners in the garden room and the outdoor bar can't help but notice the chefs and kitchen staff scuttling up the stairs to pick ingredients that momentarily will grace their dishes.

Starr's young apprentices and cooks-in-training are nourished by his commitment to using the best, freshest homegrown ingredients. In working hard and using the best food, he's inspired cooks over the years and helped launch more than his share of great master chefs.

Today, Starr Boggs, his thirty-five-seat restaurant located in West-hampton, has a loyal following of people who respect him and his culinary art. The Long Island food community and network continues to expand organically. Overall, a greater variety of produce grown is in Long Island, and Starr has been instrumental in fostering it.

Butter Lettuce Salad
with Champagne Vinaigrette

Serves 4

CHAMPAGNE VINAIGRETTE (YIELD: 1 PT.):
  1/2 c. pure olive oil
  1/2 c. champagne vinegar
  1/2 c. mayo
  2 shallots, diced
  dash Tabasco hot sauce
  salt and pepper, to taste

Emulsify all of the ingredients in a blender.

SALAD:
  2 heads butter lettuce, shredded
  4 tbsp. champagne vinaigrette
  4 tbsp. crumbled Danish blue cheese
  1 c. candied pecans
  1 Granny Smith apple, julienned

Toss the cleaned lettuce with the vinaigrette. Garnish with blue cheese crumbles, candied pecans, and julienned apple.

Softshell Crabs
with Southern Succotash

Serves 4

SOUTHERN SUCCOTASH:

- **4 slices bacon**
- **2 c. water**
- **1 c. fresh lima beans**
- **2 c. fresh corn**
- **1/2 c. Bermuda onion, diced (fine to medium)**
- **1/2 c. red pepper, diced (fine to medium)**
- **pinch black pepper**
- **pinch sugar**

Lightly render the fat from the bacon (do not brown). Add water, and cook 30 minutes. Add the lima beans, and cook until tender. Add the remaining ingredients, and cook additional 5 minutes.

CRABS:

- **8 softshell crabs, cleaned**
- **2 tbsp. flour**
- **canola oil, for frying**
- **4 tbsp. butter**
- **juice from 1/2 lemon**
- **2 c. Southern Succotash**

Lightly dredge the crabs in flour. In a sauté pan, heat canola oil over medium-high heat. Place 4 crabs in the pan, and cook for 3 to 4 minutes per side. Repeat with the remaining 4 crabs. After removing the second batch of crabs, drain the oil from the pan.

Place the butter in the pan, and brown. Pour the brown butter over the crabs. Squeeze lemon juice over the crabs. Plate the succotash, and place the crabs on top. Finish with a drizzle of brown butter from the pan.

Basil-Crusted Swordfish
with Orzo Paella

Basil-Crusted Swordfish
with Orzo Paella

Serves 4

ORZO PAELLA:

- 1/2 c. orzo pasta
- 1/2 c. chorizo sausage, diced
- 1/2 c. thawed raw shrimp, diced
- 1/2 c. fresh mussel meat
- 1/4 c. peas
- 1/4 c. scallion, sliced

Cook the orzo according to the package instructions. Sauté the chorizo. Add the shrimp, and cook through. Add the cooked orzo, mussel meat, peas, and scallions to the chorizo and shrimp; toss.

BASIL MAYO:

- 1/2 c. fresh basil leaves
- 2 tsp. olive oil
- 1 c. mayo

Purée the basil and oil in a blender. Combine with the mayo.

BASIL BREAD CRUMBS:

- 1/2 c. fresh basil leaves
- 1/4 c. fresh parsley leaves
- 1/4 c. olive oil (approximately)
- 2 c. panko bread crumbs

Blend the basil, parsley, and olive oil in a food processor until moist. Add in bread crumbs until mixed.

ROASTED PLUM TOMATOES:

- 8 plum tomatoes
- 2–3 tbsp. extra virgin olive oil
- salt and pepper, to taste

Preheat the oven to 250 degrees. Slice the tomatoes in half lengthwise. Toss with oil and a dash of salt and pepper, and then roast for 30 minutes.

SWORDFISH:

- 4 swordfish steaks, cut into 2-inch-thick pieces (approximately 8–10 oz. or 1 1/4 c.)
- 4 tbsp. Basil Mayo
- 1 c. Basil Bread Crumbs
- 4 tbsp. butter
- juice from one lemon
- 1/2 c. dry white wine
- salt and pepper
- 1/4 c. Orzo Paella
- 8 roasted plum tomatoes, cut in half

Preheat the oven to 425 degrees. Brush the top of the swordfish steaks with Basil Mayo, then coat with bread crumbs. Place the fish in a roasting pan, and top each piece with pat of butter. Add the lemon juice and enough wine to coat the bottom of the pan. Roast the fish, uncovered, until they are cooked through (approximately 18 minutes, until firm). Insert a knife into the center; if it comes out warm, the fish is done. Warm the roasted plum tomatoes by adding them to the fish for the last few minutes.

Serve the swordfish with Orzo Paella, and garnish with roasted plum tomatoes.

The North Fork and Shelter Island

The North Fork, on the upper East End of Long Island, was first settled in the 1600s and has been home for decades to duck farms and endless potato fields. Today, it boasts vineyards, oystering, farmstands, and world-class dining, and although commercial farming on nearby Shelter Island more or less ended in the 1950s, summer residents (mostly fifth- and sixth-generation families) continue to enjoy the pristine beauty of the island as well as its gourmet restaurants.

North Fork Table & Inn

Chefs Claudia Fleming and Gerry Hayden
Oysterponds Farm

Photo courtesy of Katharine Schroeder

A lot has been written about Claudia Fleming and Gerry Hayden, the husband-and-wife co-owners of the North Fork Table & Inn. She's a 2000 James Beard Award–winning pastry chef and bestselling cookbook author. He's a 2011 James Beard Best Chef nominee and earned *Esquire Magazine*'s Best Restaurant Award. But descriptions of their impressive accomplishments are usually followed by the story of how they chose to leave the bright lights of New York City to open their North Fork restaurant, modestly nestled among the vineyards and farms of Southold. Their vision helped lead what would soon become the North-Fork-as-a-culinary-destination experience.

During the second stage of a golden age that swept Gotham's restaurants in the 1980s and 1990s, Claudia joined Jonathan Waxman shortly after his 1983 return to New York from Chez Panisse to open Jams restaurant. As a struggling dancer, she worked in the front of the house merely to pay her bills. She grew up in a Long Island Italian family and explains that while they ate very well—never canned or frozen food—at Jams, her eyes were opened to ingredients she'd never seen before. Claudia found her true artistic calling in the culinary world and decided she needed some formal training. She attended Peter Kump's cooking school in Manhattan, then studied for a year in Paris at the Fauchon Patisserie.

Claudia discovered her passion for pastry when she worked at the then-groundbreaking Union Square Café. She hugs the seasons, first and foremost, parsing what's ripe and ready. When she worked with Chef Tom Collichio at Gramercy Tavern, he always told her, "If it grows together, it goes together," and she agrees. Further, her personal "Rule of Claudia" mandates that "it's OK to use a given ingredient if it comes from a region naturally and is not ever going to be available locally." She uses bananas and coffee, for example, because while they are imported to the United States, they are sourced from their native habitat.

Upon establishing their own restaurant, Claudia and Gerry had to develop ties with their growers, which Claudia says was not easy. The growers and fishermen were not used to providing products to a single source on a regular basis. There were no business terms; they wanted cash. However, they persevered and gradually built relationships on a mutually beneficial foundation, including their friendship with Tom Stevenson at Oysterponds Farm.

Tom grew up next to a ten-acre nursery in the Garden State and cared for a garden plot his dad gave him. He deepened his knowledge of growing in college before exercising his viticulture prowess at the North Shore's Osprey Dominion Vineyard for ten-plus years. In 1997, the extended family started a farm together in the town of Orient. Using the British "Haygrove Tunnel" system—with tunnels fourteen feet tall and four hundred feet long that keep birds from preying on the berries and rain from pummeling the crops—they grow their fragile crops in a protected high-yielding culture. After being introduced at a Slow Food event in 2006, Tom and Claudia forged a garden-to-table union that became a great fit for both.

Gerry shares his wife's dedication to locally grown food. Among his favorite memories from growing up in Stony Brook were his family's frequent visits to the local farmstands in Rocky Point and Wading River. Later, he and his friends worked at the source farm, harvesting the produce. At home, he helped his mother tend the family's vegetable garden and never wanted to be anything other than a chef.

His first real restaurant job at the family-owned Country House in Stony Brook left a lifelong impression. He enrolled at the Culinary Institute of America, and Chef Leon Dennon helped him secure his career-making externship with Chef Charlie Palmer at the famous River Café in Brooklyn, where he began cooking full time after graduation. Working for Palmer, Gerry felt as if he were seeing food for the first time. Palmer had grown up on a farm and adhered to a seasonally based menu.

"In a restaurant at that time, cooking according to the seasons and working directly with local food producers were both pretty new," says Gerry. There were no relationships with the growers or any of the artisans the chefs would soon help develop. Gerry says he really started getting into the farm movement when he moved to San Francisco to help open Aqua restaurant in 1990.

After several years on the West Coast, he moved back to New York and worked in the Hamptons for five years and then at TriBeCa Grill, where he met Claudia. In late June 2001, the couple catered their own wedding at the Wölfford Estate Vineyard in Bridgehampton.

Claudia and Gerry wanted to buy a home on Long Island, and it soon became clear that in the North Fork, they could have it all: the water, the local agriculture, and the community's active commitment to preserving the land. In 2005, Gerry and Claudia opened North Fork Table & Inn's 110-seat restaurant to rave reviews.

Today, the couple is dedicated to fulfilling the North Fork's potential as a food lover's paradise. They opened the restaurant here because they believe it offers the best of the culinary world's future, with the highest-quality ingredients steps away from their door. And because of their philosophy, the North Fork Table & Inn has become a food-lover's destination.

Assortment of Roasted Beets, Catapano Goat Cheese, and Roasted Pistachios

Serves 6

ROASTED BEETS:

3 bunches baby chioggia beets, leaves trimmed, washed well

3 bunches baby gold beets, leaves trimmed, washed well

3 bunches baby red beets, leaves trimmed, washed well

6 tbsp. canola oil

salt and pepper, to taste

3 cloves garlic, peeled

1 large sprig thyme

Preheat oven to 350 degrees. Place the beets in a bowl, and toss with canola oil to coat lightly. Season with salt and pepper. Place the beets in a roasting dish, reserving 1 tbsp. of the canola oil for roasting. Add the garlic cloves and thyme sprig to the roasting dish. Cover with foil, and cook until the beets are tender. The beets are done when a small knife can be easily inserted into the center of the largest beet (approximately 1 hour). Remove from the oven, take off the foil, and let cool in refrigerator.

When the beets are cool enough to handle, peel off their skin, removing just the thin outer layer. Cut the beets into quarters, place in three separate containers (one for each type), and refrigerate.

SHERRY VINAIGRETTE:

8 tbsp. sherry vinegar

pinch of salt

pinch of pepper

3/4 c. extra virgin olive oil

In a stainless steel bowl, place the sherry vinegar, salt, and pepper. Whisk in the oil.

ROASTED PISTACHIOS:

8 tbsp. pistachio nuts

1 tbsp. canola oil, reserved from roasted beets

2 tbsp. fleur de sel (sea salt)

In a bowl, place the pistachio nuts and reserved 1 tbsp. canola oil. Toss and season with fleur de sel. Place on a baking sheet, and bake until pistachios are well toasted (about 4 to 5 minutes).

ASSEMBLY:

salt and pepper, to taste

1 lb. fresh Catapano Dairy Farm goat cheese

1/4 c. pistachio oil

2 tbsp. micro amaranth, to be used as garnish (no cooking)

fleur de sel (sea salt), to taste

In three separate bowls, toss each of the three types of beets in its own bowl with a generous amount of Sherry Vinaigrette and season with salt and pepper. Arrange on a large oval platter, layering the three beet types to get a nice blending of colors. Crumble goat cheese over the top of the beets, top with Roasted Pistachios, and drizzle pistachio oil over the top. Garnish with amaranth and fleur de sel.

Assortment of Roasted Beets, Catapano Goat Cheese & Roasted Pistachios

Roasted Curried Butternut Squash and Crispin Apple Soup

Serves 6

1 butternut squash, about 2 lb. (a 2 lb. butternut squash
  raw should yield 1 lb. after roasting)
3 tbsp. butter
kosher salt and freshly ground white pepper, to taste
1/4 lb. white onion, sliced
2 Crispin apples, peeled and sliced (Granny Smith or Mutsu
  may be substituted)
1 tbsp. fresh ginger, peeled and sliced thin
1 tbsp. Madras curry powder
1 tbsp. fresh thyme leaves
1 vanilla bean, split and scraped
1 ripe banana, peeled and mashed
1 tsp. olive or vegetable oil

Preheat the oven to 350 degrees. Split the squash lengthwise, and
scoop out seeds, reserving them in a bowl. Wash the squash halves
well, and dry. Rub the flesh of the squash with 1 tbsp. butter, and
season it with salt and pepper. Place on a baking sheet, cut side
down, and roast in the oven until the flesh is soft (approximately 1
1/2 hours).

Scoop the flesh from the skin of the squash, and reserve. In a
heavy-bottomed, large saucepot, over medium-high heat, melt the
remaining 2 tbsp. butter. Add the onions, and cook until soft (about
3 minutes). Add the apples, ginger, roasted squash, curry powder,
thyme, and vanilla bean. Lower the heat, and cook for 15 minutes,
until all of the ingredients are softened.

Add the banana, and cover with water 1 inch above ingredients.
Simmer for another 20 minutes. Remove the vanilla bean. In small
batches, blend the mixture in a blender until it is very smooth. Add
more salt and pepper, if needed.

Toss the reserved squash seeds in a bowl with a teaspoon of cooking oil. Place on a baking sheet, and sprinkle with salt. Roast in an
oven until golden brown.

Divide the soup into soup bowls, and garnish with roasted seeds.
Serve immediately.

Blueberry Cobbler

Serves 6–8

COBBLER DOUGH:

- 1 2/3 c. all purpose flour
- 3 1/2 tbsp. sugar
- 1 1/2 tbsp. baking powder
- 1/8 tsp. salt
- 6 tbsp. (3 oz.) very cold unsalted butter, cut into
  1/2-inch pieces
- 2 hard-boiled egg yolks
- 2/3 c. plus 2 tbsp. very cold heavy cream
- 2 tbsp. turbinado sugar

Preheat oven to 350 degrees. In the bowl of a food processor, combine the flour, sugar, baking powder, salt, and hard-boiled egg yolks. Pulse to combine, until the yolks are broken down. Add very cold butter; mix until the dough resembles fine meal. Add the cream, and pulse until the dough just comes together. Turn the dough out onto a lightly floured board, gently gather the dough into a mass (the dough needn't be smooth). Using a large spoon dipped in flour, form dough into 8 to 10 2-inch shaped balls. Chill for 30 minutes or up to 8 hours.

PEACH-BLUEBERRY FILLING:

- 2 lb. sliced, fresh peaches
- 1 lb. blueberries
- 6 tbsp. granulated sugar

In a large bowl, toss together the peaches, blueberries, and sugar. Put the fruit in a shallow 2 1/2-qt. baking dish. Arrange the 2-inch dough ball biscuits on top, leaving approximately 1 inch between them. Brush the biscuits with the remaining 2 tbsp. of cream, and sprinkle with the turbinado sugar. Bake the cobbler until the fruit is bubbling and the biscuits are golden brown (30 to 40 minutes).

Jedediah Hawkins Inn

Chef Keith Luce

Jedediah Hawkins Inn Garden

For a kid who grew up on his family's twenty-plus-acre farm in nearby Riverhead, it's ironic that great *houses* have figured prominently in Chef Keith Luce's success. First there was the White House. Yes, the grand one with the 1600 Pennsylvania Avenue address. Now there is the stately Jedediah Hawkins Inn in Jamesport.

Promoting itself as "built in 1863, restored in 2005," the remodel turned the Italianate-style historic home into a working inn and restaurant that garnered the New York State Historic Preservation Office's Project Achievement Award in 2008 and a spot on the National Register of Historic Places. The inn's restaurant is now dedicated to providing a locally sourced menu, boasting how patrons can enjoy "the local bounty while participating in the culture and heritage of the North Fork."

Keith's family history in the area goes back further than the inn's; his ancestors came to Luce's Landing in the 1600s. Growing up not three miles from the inn, he remembers the house of seafaring Captain Jedediah Hawkins' homestead looking more like a haunted house then a sophisticated destination.

After first pursuing a musical career, Keith was able to discover and unleash his culinary artistic talent with the help of his mentor, Jean-Jacques Rachou, the influential chef and owner of New York City's La Cote Basque, where Keith worked early in his career. Rachou was well known for his elegant and traditional classic French haute cuisine, and he urged Keith to go to Europe to study cooking. With Rachou opening doors for him, Keith spent two years working in some of the best kitchens in Paris, Strasbourg, and Italy.

In 1989, before leaving for Europe, Keith worked at the famed five-diamond Greenbrier resort in West Virginia. There, he made an impression on executive chef Walter Scheib—so good, in fact, that upon Keith's return to the United States in 1991, Scheib invited him to work at his new venue: the White House. Keith became the youngest sous chef ever to serve in the executive residence, helping create great American menus there until 1995.

Since then, during the course of his acclaimed career, Keith has been hailed for his work at the Rainbow Room and Le Cirque, as well as for his award-winning cooking at the Herbfarm in Washington State. He was named a top-ten chef by *Food & Wine* magazine in 1997, and a year later was honored with a coveted James Beard Award as a rising star. He's also appeared on the TV show *Top Chef* as a guest judge.

In 2010, he realized it was time to return to Long Island to live the good life with his young family. Becoming an innkeeper was a bit of kismet.

"I met my partner after a deal that I was working on in Greenport fell through. I loved the idea of taking on the challenge of an inn and restaurant—which was always my dream. The fact that the property was restored, historically important, and so near my family's homestead made the deal that much sweeter!"

As Keith says, "For me, this is an extremely personal project. This isn't just about an inn and a restaurant; it's about the region and the community. It's my home."

At the inn's thirty-six-seat restaurant, Keith starts the day cooking breakfast with farm-fresh eggs from the inn's chickens, which are raised behind the building, and baking fresh bread in the Wood Stone fire oven. After breakfast, he'll chat with the inn's guests at the dining table or in one of the sitting rooms about the previous night's dinner, the local vineyards, and what's coming up in his garden out back. Farm-to-table doesn't get any fresher. He harvests vegetables and fruits from the inn's kitchen garden to serve immediately. He'll also stop by the local farmstands and pick up whatever else he may need—or be seduced by—before heading back to the inn to prepare for dinner.

The newly installed potager garden was designed and put in by Keith, his father, and his employee, Fernando Chos, the first spring the inn reopened. The three did about eighteen months of work in four months, Keith recounts with exhausted pride. The edible garden is planted behind the kitchen so Keith and his cooks can run out to pinch this herb or snip those beans to use readily in his cooking. He designed the beds himself and drew up the plan for positioning the row crops. The paths and mulch in the garden are beautiful, caramel-colored spent hazelnut shells he has sent in from his Northwest farm friends, Holmquist Hazelnut Orchards.

In addition to raising chickens and vegetables, Keith and his kitchen team make the inn's salt from the local seawater of Peconic Bay, Long Island Sound, and the Atlantic Ocean. The seawater is heated on the stove, then strained and restrained over cheesecloth into a pot. Twenty-five gallons of water yields only a pint of salt, but the effort is worth it, because, as Keith explains, the salt has a fantastic local taste.

When designing his garden, Keith laid it out in quadrants specifically to entice guests to walk through and enjoy it. Keith proudly notes the garden itself has become an attraction. Some people come to the inn for cocktails, an appetizer, and a romantic garden walk.

Apple Rosemary Fritters

Serves 4–6

1 tbsp. butter
2 tbsp. brown sugar
juice of one lemon
1/4 c. water
2 c. chopped apples
splash of apple brandy
1/4 c. finely chopped rosemary
2 eggs, separated
2/3 c. milk
1 tbsp. butter, melted
1 c. sifted flour
1/4 tsp. salt
1 tbsp. sugar
1/4 tsp. cinnamon
confectioners' sugar, for dusting
oil, for frying

Preheat a deep fryer. In a saucepan, melt the butter. Stir in the brown sugar, and cook for 30 seconds to dissolve the sugar. Add the lemon juice, water, apples, brandy, and rosemary. Cook the apples for about 3 to 5 minutes or until the apples start to wilt. Remove from the heat, and cool completely.

In a mixing bowl, whisk the egg yolks, milk, melted butter, and cooled apple mixture. Stir the dry ingredients (except for the confectioners' sugar) into the liquid mixture. Blend until the batter is incorporated. Cover the batter, place in the refrigerator, and let rest for 2 to 4 hours.

In a standing mixer or with a whisk, beat the egg whites until stiff. Remove the batter from the refrigerator, and blend until smooth. Fold in the beaten egg white. Using a large spoon, drop the batter into the hot oil and fry until golden brown (about 3 to 4 minutes). Remove from the oil, and drain on a paper-lined plate.

Boulangere Potatoes
with Purple Sage

Serves 4–6

6 oz. bacon, cut into lardons (a small matchstick-sized strip or cube of bacon or pork belly fat, approximately 1/4 inch thick)

2 garlic cloves, chopped

2 sweet onions, chopped

7 juniper berries, crushed

3 tbsp. thyme leaves

1/4 c. fresh purple sage, chopped

1/4 c. parsley, chopped

6 lb. potatoes (baking), peeled and cut about 1/8 inch thick

1 qt. meat stock

1 qt. chicken stock

1/2 c. butter, cut in small pieces

Brown the bacon lightly. Add the garlic, juniper berries, and onions, and cook until softened. Add the herbs (thyme, sage, and parsley).

Place the potatoes in buttered pans, top with the bacon herb mix, cover with stock, and top with butter. Season and bake covered until tender. Uncover and cook in the oven until the top is brown and slightly crisp.

Stout BBQ Sauce

Serves 4–6

1/2 c. (or a little less) vegetable oil

4 onions, diced small

5 c. tomato purée

1 qt. (or 1 L) stout beer (approximately)

1 c. molasses

3 1/2 oz. cider vinegar

1/4 c. brown sugar (packed)

salt, to taste

Heat the oil in a medium sauce pot, and sweat onions until translucent (cook gently with a lid on low-medium to low heat). Add all other ingredients, and simmer gently for 1 to 2 hours. Be sure to stir the bottom of the pot often to avoid burning. Slather on your favorite ribs, steaks, and chops.

Satur Farms

Chef Eberhard Müller

Satur Farms

Chef Eberhard Müller had already had a long and storied career when he realized something was missing.

In his native Germany, he began his formal culinary apprenticeship within the guild-like European professional training system at the impossibly young age of thirteen. After completing a three-year program combining cooking and studies, he worked in various restaurants in and around the Black Forest area and in Switzerland and made his pilgrimage to Paris. For six years, he worked at L'Archestrate, a three-star Michelin restaurant, and traveled all over the world with the restaurant owner, conducting cooking events at local restaurants and private parties.

In 1982, Eberhard became executive chef at the Windows on the World restaurant at the top of the World Trade Center before moving to the newly opened, now-legendary restaurant Le Bernardin as executive chef. After opening his own restaurant in Los Angeles in the early 1990s, he returned to New York to take over the heart-stopping culinary apogee Lutece. He remained at the helm for six years before becoming a partner and executive chef at Bayard's restaurant, in Manhattan's financial district.

But despite four-star reviews, and legions of loyal fans, Eberhard was dissatisfied with the food that composed his culinary-art palette. In Paris, he and his fellow European culinary artists had been taught to visit the small garden markets for their ingredients. So naturally, they wanted to do the same in New York City. Unfortunately, it wasn't available. Adding insult to injury, the end-of-the-century culinary zeitgeist said food ingredients were sexy only if they were imported. Truffles from Italy? No problem. Foie gras from France? You bet.

There were few locally grown farmers' markets in New York in those days, and those that sprouted up were too nascent to have any real impact on restaurants' menus. So Eberhard and his fellow European chefs banded together to find small farms and gardens that would supply them with products they needed and wanted. They did the best they could, but the quality of available products just wasn't up to their exacting standards.

Meanwhile, in 1996, while he was cooking at Lutece, Eberhard and his fiancée, Paulette Satur, decided to buy a country place on the North Fork of Long Island. In 1997, they purchased eighteen acres of a former potato farm, built a house, and started gardening on a quarter of an acre there. He learned a lot on the farm and from his wife, who'd grown up on a dairy farm in Pennsylvania, studied horticulture at Pennsylvania State, and earned a master's degree in plant physiology from the University of Arizona.

The vegetables and fruits he brought from their weekend garden to his kitchen at Lutece completely changed his menu. His European chef associates started to notice and would beg him to bring them some garden-fresh food too. Paulette, an account representative for a Long Island wine importer, then began getting requests from her restaurant customers.

To satisfy the increasing demand, the two began harvesting more and more garden edibles, including rare and exotic local produce like micro greens and squash blossoms. Soon, Satur Farms was not only growing organic produce and selling to major restaurants on Long Island and in Manhattan, but it was selling Satur-brand products to Whole Foods, a then-new business concept.

The North Fork property is now more than 180 acres. Following their initial success, Eberhard and Paulette soon expanded to a winter farm and have replicated their Long Island model in Florida, growing produce on about 140 acres there.

Eberhard laughs when he says he didn't realize how much work farming was. And because of Eberhard's perspective as a chef, the two know that if they aren't producing and delivering clean, delicious food on schedule, they will be out of business in the time it takes a waiter to run down the specials of the day.

The couple's ability to assess their clients' needs accurately is due to the extraordinary, unmatched relationships they've established with their customers. Some chefs ask Satur Farms to grow certain edibles; others rely on the farm to inspire them.

Every day, fleets of Satur trucks leave the bucolic North Fork farm to deliver to wholesale and retail accounts in New York, Connecticut, and New Jersey. They deliver directly to accounts such as Whole Foods, Food Emporium, Dean & DeLuca, and Fairway. And they continue to supply Fresh Direct, their first retail account. Looking ahead, Eberhard believes the interest in a sustainable lifestyle will continue, saying there is a huge future market for locally grown fresh foods.

"We realize we can't eat just more foods," he says. "We need to eat more variety of quality food."

Eberhard explains why he chose to trade in his toque for a tractor by quoting George Bernard Shaw: "The reasonable man adapts himself to the world, the unreasonable one persists in trying to adapt the world to himself. Therefore, all progress depends on the unreasonable man." He jokes that he is that unreasonable man. But another quote from Shaw could easily explain his decision: "There is no love sincerer than the love of food."

Spiced Fish and Vegetable Stew with Basil

Serves 4

This dish can be made with any firm cooking fish and any combination of vegetables that are really fresh and in season. In this version, I am using black sea bass and baby pak choi. Baby vegetables are readily available to me, but you can use regular-size vegetables cut to size. The broth is basically water, but you can add some chicken stock. If you do so, be sure it does not overpower the vegetable and fish flavor.

3 1/2 c. water

1/2 c. chicken stock (optional)

3 Yukon Gold potatoes, peeled and diced in 1/4-inch pieces

1 small onion, peeled and julienned

12 baby carrots (different colors if available), peeled and trimmed

1 small jalapeño pepper, seeded and sliced finely

2 stalks celery, peeled and sliced

4 pieces black bass filets, about 5 oz. each, deboned and skinned

2 c. mussels

salt and pepper

8 pieces baby pak choi, cleaned and trimmed

2 medium tomatoes, peeled, seeded, and cut in 1/2-inch cubes

1/2 c. basil leaves, julienned

In a pan large enough to hold all the ingredients, bring the water and chicken stock to a boil. Add the diced potatoes and julienned onion. Bring to a slow boil, and simmer covered for 10 minutes. Add the baby carrots, jalapeño pepper, and celery, and simmer covered for 8 minutes more.

Season the fish filets with salt and pepper. Add the fish, mussels, baby pak choi, and tomatoes to the simmering broth. Cover and simmer for 3 to 5 minutes.

Add the basil julienne, and let steep for 2 minutes or until the mussels have opened. Check the seasoning, and adjust as necessary. Serve immediately.

Monkfish with Stewed Leeks

Serves 4–6

6 medium-sized leeks
2 lb. monkfish filet
salt
pepper from a mill
1 tbsp. all-purpose flour
1 tbsp. vegetable oil
water, to cover the leeks for cooking
6 tbsp. sweet butter
juice from 1/2 lemon
1 tbsp. chives, minced

Preheat the oven to 350 degrees. Wash the leeks, and cut off the root ends and tough green leaves. Cut in half lengthwise, then slice thinly crosswise. Wash thoroughly in a big bowl of water, and drain.

Trim the fish, removing any fatty tissue and membrane (which will toughen the fish if left on). Pat dry with a paper towel, and season with salt and a few generous turns of the pepper mill. Sprinkle evenly with flour.

Using a large, heavy skillet, heat the vegetable oil. When it starts to smoke ever so slightly, place the monkfish filets in the skillet and brown them on all sides. If the filets are large, finish cooking them by putting them in the oven for a few minutes.

In a pot large enough to fit the sliced leeks, heat the water and 3 tbsp. of the butter. Season with salt and pepper from the mill. Add the leeks, and steam over moderate heat until they are tender but still have a nice green color. Add the remaining butter, and stir until melted and well blended. Add a few drops of lemon juice and the minced chives. Check the seasoning.

Slice the monkfish evenly, and serve over a bed of the stewed leeks.

Tuna Tartar
with Three Spring Radishes

Serves 6 as an appetizer, 4 as a main course

The radishes used in this recipe are those typically in season at Satur Farm. Any slightly spicy and crunchy radish can be substituted for them.

3/4 lb. sushi-grade tuna

1 small bunch French breakfast radishes

1 small bunch white icicle radishes

1 small bunch shunkyo radishes

salt

juice of 2 limes

2 1/2 tbsp. extra virgin olive oil

1/4 tbsp. freshly grated horseradish, or a small dollop
   Japanese horseradish (wasabi)

1/2 tbsp. chives, minced

1/2 tsp. coarse sea salt (fleur de sel or similar)

black pepper from a mill

2 oz. China rose radish shoots

Cut the tuna into even 1/8-inch dices, and chill for 1 hour. Cut off and discard the radish tops. Julienne the radishes. (You should have 1 1/2 c. radish julienne.) Lightly salt the radish julienne, and sprinkle with a few drops of lime juice.

Combine the diced tuna, the radish julienne, 2 tsp. olive oil, the juice from 1 1/2 limes, the horseradish, the chives, and the coarse sea salt. Season generously with black pepper from the mill. Mix thoroughly and check the seasoning, adjusting as necessary.

Season the China rose radish shoots with the remaining olive oil, lime juice, and salt and pepper. Place the tuna tartar on a chilled platter, and dress the radish shoots around it.

Cuvée Bistro & Bar, Greenporter Hotel

Chef Deborah Pittorino
Aeros Cultured Oyster Company and Noank
Aquaculture Cooperative

While always a cook, Deborah never imagined she'd become a professional chef. Growing up, she probably spent more time in the kitchen than most kids. But then, food—and its preparation and consumption—was in many ways an escape from Deborah's childhood family dynamics.

Deborah's father was a diplomat in the U.S. State Department, and after her parents' divorce, time with her father was spent traveling and living in exotic locales like India, Spain, and Madagascar. Cooking and food, along with the safe haven of time spent with the embassy cooks in the kitchens wherever her father was posted, provided solace.

Back home in the Midwest with her mother and grandmother, she learned the joy of cooking recipes handed down from her family (Spanish by way of Puerto Rico), as well as local, all-American foods. With cheerful enthusiasm she learned gardening in their edible, three-season potager. But among these disparate family experiences, food was the common thread with striking power. Both parents ingrained within Deborah old-world values of hard work and discipline. Today, Deborah manages a global business (The Succession Group) while serving as weekend innkeeper, head gardener, and executive chef as well.

How did she come to own a restaurant and an expanding hotel while managing a financial recruiting business at the same time?

It all started with summers spent in the Hamptons as "a young single woman at those fabulous South Fork parties in the summer and loft parties in Manhattan." At one of those soirees, she met her husband, William. They married in August 1999, and it wasn't long before they set out looking for a country home on the North Fork.

They couldn't seem to find a place they liked until Deborah saw what was then a sagging motor lodge property that looked like it was pining for its Jimmy Carter–era heyday and, with her inimitable vision, saw what it *could* be. To her surprise, she found herself putting a bid on it. The couple opened the hotel in July 2001, then added the restaurant in March 2002 and another wing to the hotel in 2004.

Deborah learned how to cook from true craftsmen around the world, firsthand, and from her family experiences. She is a stickler for consistency and quality, but that's not to say she doesn't create head-smacking, innovative dishes that are flavor knockouts. And she does so with a sophisticated and informed knowledge of culinary culture and a respect for the food and farm process.

How does she do it all? During the week, Deborah is up before dawn with calls at 4 a.m. to Europe. On Fridays, she runs to catch the Hampton Jitney in Midtown Manhattan, stopping at the farmers' markets in the city before heading out. "I might think I'm so tired but then I get to the restaurant and the juices start flowing!" she says.

Locally, she's built food relationships that, like a spider web, extend out from existing, key connections. "The clamming guy sees me from his fishing boat and figures I'm OK. He tells the tomato farmer, and so on. Word gets around," she says smartly.

Her favorite oyster farmer is Karen Rivara, a marine scientist who, after completing a research project in 1981 at the first oyster hatchery in the area (located on the Shinnecock Indian reservation), launched Aeros hatchery with Jim Markow in 1992. They purchased old oyster beds off the Ram Island coast and developed the Noank Aquaculture Cooperative, continuing a one-hundred-year heritage of growing oysters utilizing traditional farming methods while pursuing new, sustainable business operations. Karen moved the hatchery to Shellfisher Preserve, a Peconic Land Trust property, and now farms two brands of the native Eastern Oyster from their own seed: Peconic Pearls® and Mystic Oyster. Customers are willing to pay a little extra for the Peconic Pearls to benefit the Peconic Bay estuary. Karen and Deborah met at a Slow Food fundraiser, and shortly thereafter, Cuvée earned the distinction of becoming the first restaurant to work with Aeros.

For most comestibles, Deborah would rather grow them herself, but when her own garden proved not big enough to handle her needs, she turned to Mike Ficurelli, a neighbor with a big garden. "Mike's brother is a barber that my husband goes to. He said if we ever needed anything, to just go pick some stuff at his brother's," Deborah relates. "So I was in a pinch one weekend and marched over." Not finding anyone there, Deborah started filling her basket with some lovely Lebanese eggplant when all of a sudden she heard someone shouting, "Hey!" Now she and Mike work as a team in the Cuvée restaurant garden.

Deborah composts from her restaurant kitchen, of course. She also cans and preserves the garden harvest, such as those juicy Long Island tomatoes. The vegetables and fruits she puts up from the plentiful growing season, along with the abundance of seasonal fish, allow her to overcome creatively the chef's lament, "There's nothing local to serve this time of year." Besides, she adds mischievously, "I love changing perceptions."

Did she see the move to local, sustainable food coming? "I did feel it was going to happen. . . . People are aware of food sources, and I want to enlighten people about the Long Island back-to-the-land devotion and about the fact that I grow so much of the food served here."

Farmstand Strawberry-Rhubarb Tartelettes

Serves 8

CRUST:

- 3/4 c. plain flour
- pinch of salt
- 3 oz. unsalted butter, slightly softened
- 2 egg yolks
- 1 tbsp. cold water
- 1 1/2 oz. caster sugar

Sift the flour and salt into a pile on a cold work surface, and make a well in the center. Add the butter, egg yolks, water, and sugar to the well, and use the fingertips of one hand to work them together into a rough paste. The mixture should resemble scrambled eggs. Gradually work in the flour with your fingertips to bind the mixture into smooth dough. Press together lightly, and form into a ball. Wrap in plastic wrap, and chill for about 30 minutes before use.

FILLING:

- 2 c. fresh strawberries, sliced and divided
- 4 tbsp. cassis
- 2 c. fresh rhubarb, diced
- 1/4 c. sugar
- 1/2 tbsp. freshly grated lemon zest
- 1 1/2 tbsp. cornstarch
- 1 tbsp. rose syrup

Hull and slice the berries. Irregular pieces work best, as they look better than a bunch of nearly identical slices. Mash a few of the berries, if you wish, and toss them with the remaining berries in a large bowl. Add the cassis on top of the berries, and stir gently to coat them. Refrigerate for at least 2 hours.

Combine the rhubarb, sugar, and lemon zest in a large nonreactive saucepan. Let stand for 20 minutes. Bring the mixture to a simmer over medium-low heat. Cook, stirring often, until the rhubarb is tender but still holds its shape (5 to 8 minutes).

Meanwhile, stir the cornstarch and rose syrup in a small bowl until smooth. Stir into the simmering fruit. Cook, stirring constantly, until the mixture is clear and very thick (about 1 minute). Transfer to a bowl. Place a piece of plastic wrap directly on the surface, and refrigerate until chilled.

STRAWBERRY-BALSAMIC GASTRIQUE:

- 3/4 c. superfine sugar
- 3/4 c. hot water
- 1 c. strawberries, halved, hulled, and puréed
- 1/2 c. balsamic vinegar

In a medium saucepan, stir the sugar into the hot water until dissolved. Add the strawberries, and simmer over low heat for 30 minutes. Add the balsamic vinegar, increase the heat, and bring to a boil. Next, reduce the heat to low, and simmer until thickened (about 30 minutes). Let the gastrique cool, then strain it into a jar, cover, and refrigerate.

Assembling the tarts: Preheat the oven to 400 degrees. Divide the dough into eight balls. Roll out each ball to fill the tart pans. Remove excess dough from edges, reserving it for the lattice work. Divide the filling into eight sections and fill each pan. Be careful not to overfill, or it will spill out during baking. With the excess dough, create a lattice on top of the pie. Brush the lattice with melted butter, as it will prevent burning and give each tart a golden color.

Bake the tarts for 25 to 30 minutes until the crust is a golden color and the juices are bubbling. Remove from the oven, and place on a cooling rack. Allow the tarts to reach room temperature before serving. Serve each tart with some vanilla ice cream and a drizzle of the Strawberry-Balsamic Gastrique.

Cuvée Oysters

Serving size: 12 Cuvée oysters

"Out East" we are at the center of shellfish farming, propelled by Cornell University's agricultural extension in Riverhead—where the North Fork begins. With my restaurant in Greenport, I am a fortunate recipient of this movement with access to some of the best oysters on the East Coast. I designed a recipe to showcase these oysters on our menu and sure enough, it's one of our top-selling appetizers.

FRIED OYSTERS:

12 oysters, opened and refrigerated

1/2 qt. canola oil, for frying, heated to 375 degrees

1/2 c. flour for dredging

2 eggs beaten with 1 tbsp. of water

1/2 c. breadcrumbs

Use a larger oyster when flash frying to get crispier outer mass and a center that remains creamy. Save the bottom shells, rinse and dry for serving. Use a large cast-iron Dutch oven or similar pot for frying. Set up a breading area or station: flour for dredging, egg wash, and your favorite bread crumbs. Drop each oyster into the flour, then the egg wash, then place each coated oyster on large plate or cookie sheet; refrigerate until all are ready to fry.

SPINACH:

1 tsp. olive oil (for sautéing)

1 c. baby spinach

pinch of salt

Add the olive oil to the pan with the spinach and sauté. Add a pinch of salt. There should be enough spinach to place a teaspoon of spinach at the bottom or inside of each cleaned oyster shell when ready to serve.

SAUCE:

2 tbsp. shallots, finely minced

1/8 c. olive oil

1/2 c. Verjus (I use nearby Wolffer Estates)

1 knob of butter (approximately 2 tbsp.)

1/4 c. heavy cream

salt and pepper, to taste

Sauté the shallots, and once the shallots are transparent, add the Verjus to the pan and begin to reduce at medium heat (approximately 5 to 7 minutes). Once halfway reduced, add the heavy cream and simmer. Season with salt to taste and a pinch of white pepper. Add the butter at the end, stirring until the butter is dissolved and the sauce is glistening. Set the sauce aside, and refrigerate until ready to use. You may have extra, which is fine because this sauce is great on grilled fish or vegetables.

To assemble: When ready to serve, heat the pan with canola oil to 375 degrees and flash fry the oysters. Place them on a plate or screen to absorb extra oil. Choose a beautiful platter to display these oysters. I usually line my platter with wild fennel from my garden. Place shells on the platter with your garnish. These oysters are delicious with a bottle of crisp Chardonnay from Bedell Cellars.

Arugula Pesto with Pasta

Serves 4

Arugula pesto is much milder than the traditional basil pesto and, therefore, more versatile in everyday recipes.

PESTO:

  2 c. fresh arugula, washed and dried
  1 clove garlic, smashed and finely minced
  2 tbsp. pine nuts
  1/4 c. grated, high-quality Parmesan cheese
  1/4 c. extra virgin olive oil

PASTA:

  1/2 lb. orrechiette pasta
  1 tbsp. extra virgin olive oil
  1/2 c. grape or cherry tomatoes
  1/2 c. half and half (or heavy cream)
  2 heaping tbsp. arugula pesto
  1 tbsp. high-quality Parmesan cheese
  pine nuts or walnuts to garnish

Cook 1/2 lb. orrechiette al dente, and set aside.

Place the arugula, garlic, pine nuts, and Parmesan cheese in the food processor, and drizzle in olive oil while using the pulse setting. Continue using the pulse setting until the mixture becomes a thick paste and you can still see bits of arugula leaf and pine nuts. Pulsing more than eight times will cause the mixture to become over-processed. If the pesto is too thick, add olive oil; if too thin, add a few more leaves of arugula and pulse one to two times more. Do not add salt to the mixture until after tasting, as the Parmesan cheese is salty. Pesto can be stored in canning jars or plastic containers in the refrigerator for up to 3 months.

Add 1 tbsp. extra virgin olive oil to a sauté pan, along with 1/2 c. sliced grape or cherry tomatoes; flash sauté. Then pour in 1/2 c. half and half (or heavy cream), and quickly add 2 heaping tbsp. pesto. Add the al dente orrechiette and 1 tbsp. high-quality Parmesan cheese, and then turn off your flame. Only heat the pesto, don't cook it. Cooking it too long will alter the vibrant green color. Taste for flavor. You may want to add more cream or pesto for a creamier consistency. Serve immediately, garnishing with a slight sprinkle of cheese and some pine nuts or walnuts.

The Frisky Oyster

Chef Robby Beaver

KK's "The Farm"

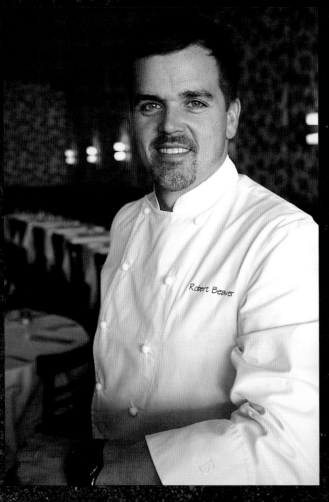

The grandson of Virginia tobacco farmers, Chef Robby Beaver can trace his agricultural roots across generations. Robby enjoyed the double-dip privilege of cooking and gardening with his mother and grandmother while also working with his father in the family's expanding landscape business. But for the culinary thrill of working with the bounty of the edible garden, he too might be carrying on the family tradition of working the land.

Robby's culinary christening occurred as a teenager, when he took a surf and turf restaurant job for extra cash. After quickly moving up from dishwasher and salad prep to the grill, Robby's heart sank when a guest came back to the kitchen demanding to know "Who cooked my steak?" Much to his surprise, the man handed him a twenty-dollar bill and said, "Thank you for the best steak I've ever had." It was then this future "pasture to plate" chef discovered he wanted to cook professionally.

Later, while Robby was working full time at a Ruth's Chris Steak House, observant restaurant manager Steve Parry saw something in the diligent cook and networked Robby to Jeff Buben, owner and executive chef of Vidalia and Bistro Bis in Washington DC. An awestruck Robby would arrive more than three hours before he needed to report for work just to watch Jeff prepare that night's menu. Robby respected Jeff's extraordinary work ethic as well as his dual devotional lifestyle: to his two restaurants and to his family.

After two years of learning fundamentals, Robby enrolled at the Culinary Institute of America (CIA) in 2001 to gain formal training. With cool conviction and an eye toward maximizing the learning experience, he chose to do his externship at nearby Mohonk Mountain House, a year-round, high-volume, top-quality entertainment resort.

In addition, the CIA awarded Robby the prestigious fellowship and chose him to be sous chef at its in-house Italian restaurant, Catarina de Medici, following graduation. He then returned to Virginia with one goal: to work at the Inn at Little Washington.

The application process was a two-day ordeal, and at the end of day two, he learned, to his astounded surprise, that he would have a mere hour to prepare a meal for Chef Patrick O'Connell. He was told, "You can use anything within the restaurant." He was understandably nervous. "I went into one of the two walk-ins: there was fresh lobster, foie gras, caviar." But then instinct and the budding culinary prophet in Robby turned around to the other, produce-laden walk-in. "I was thinking, 'Everyone tries to wow using fancy ingredients to show off their talent.'" He strategically chose to do a fresh herb green salad.

The nest of crispy parsnips and celeriac and jalapeños topped off with nectarines took him almost a full hour to chop and arrange just so, constructing a masterful plating to present. The judgment was soon rendered. Robby aced the interview.

Robby worked at the inn for three years, but after the birth of their first child, he and his wife decided to move to Long Island to be closer

to family. He didn't have a job, but eventually a friend connected Robby with Hank Tomashevski, then a co-owner of the Frisky Oyster. Robby was hired as the executive chef, working three years until he bought the restaurant in late 2008.

Robby's country gentleman manners suited the locals just fine. "Farmers here are into talking about what you're doing. Everyone is seeking out great partners and into building relationships," explains Robby. A key partnership for Robby is with KK Haspel and her biodynamic farm.

When KK (Kathy Keller) and her husband, Ira, began looking for a second home on the North Fork, all they wanted was a barn, a hammock, and no phone. But nothing they saw for a year met their expectations until they found what is now "The Farm."

There was no mistaking KK's immediate, kinetic connection to the land and to her flowers and vegetables. Following local tradition, she put out the "extras" on a stand at the end of the driveway, where people could hardly get enough. At the same time, she enrolled in a two-day intensive course on organics and biodynamics in West Hampton.

Everything at The Farm is grown in fifty to seventy tons of biodynamic topsoil, which KK explains will create twelve inches of topsoil a year and help produce last longer by two to three weeks. The microbiotics in the soil make for a unique and powerful food source. Emblematic of KK's devoted chef following is her connection with Robby, who frequents The Farm, tasting this and that, drawing his inspiration from walking the field together with KK.

Robby includes the names of the farmers, fishermen, and local food artisans on the menu. "It's important to me to show that provenance to my customers. Almost everyone interested in fine dining wants to know where their food comes from," he adds.

Robby's guidelines to sourcing food are to use ingredients within two hundred miles of the Frisky Oyster. In the summer season, that geographic radius narrows down considerably, he reports.

Robby believes the return to homegrown cooking will continue. "Being here is exactly where I want to be. I couldn't imagine being as successful and as satisfied anywhere else." Essentially, Robby continues the family tradition of "working the land" his way.

Roasted Baby Beet Salad with Humboldt Fog Goat Cheese

Makes 4 salads

BEETS:

- **10 baby red beets**
- **10 baby golden beets**
- **10 baby candy stripe beets**
- **1 bunch fresh thyme**
- **1 c. extra virgin olive oil**
- **2 c. balsamic vinegar**

Place the beets, thyme, oil, and vinegar in a baking dish, and cover with aluminum foil. Bake at 375 degrees until a toothpick or knife slides into and out of the beets with little resistance. Uncover and allow to cool in the cooking liquid, then refrigerate for several hours or until cold. Remove the beets from the liquid and peel each one, removing any peel around the stem end. Cut in half and set aside.

PISTACHIOS:

- **1 c. pistachios, raw**
- **1 tbsp. butter**
- **1 tsp. salt**
- **1 tsp. sugar**

Place the pistachios on a baking sheet, and put them in a 375-degree oven to toast for 8 to 10 minutes. While they are cooking, heat a small sauté pan on a high flame. Add the butter and swirl, remove from the heat, and reserve for the nuts. When the pistachios are done, place them in a mixing bowl. Add the brown butter, salt, and sugar, and toss to coat evenly. Set the nuts aside, and allow them to cool to room temperature.

SHERRY VINAIGRETTE:

- **2 tbsp. Dijon mustard**
- **1 shallot, chopped**
- **2 cloves garlic, chopped**
- **2 tbsp. dry sherry**
- **5 oz. sherry vinegar**
- **1 c. canola or neutral salad oil**
- **1/2 c. pure olive oil**
- **3 tbsp. walnut oil**
- **salt and fresh black pepper, to taste**

Place all of the ingredients except the oils and the salt and pepper in a blender, and process on high. Slowly stream in the oils, one at a time, until the vinaigrette is smooth. Season to taste with salt and pepper.

TO SERVE:

- **roasted baby beets**
- **1 lb. baby arugula (best fresh from a local organic farm)**
- **1/2 c. Sherry Vinaigrette**
- **4 slices Humboldt Fog goat's milk cheese (or your favorite goat's milk cheese)**
- **1 c. salted pistachios**

Arrange the beets on each plate, and drizzle with Sherry Vinaigrette. Toss the baby arugula in a bowl with the vinaigrette, and place a handful on each plate. Garnish with a slice of Humboldt Fog goat's milk cheese and pistachios.

Grilled Local Striped Bass with Six Spices and KK's Great White Tomatoes

Serves 6

BASS:

**1 tbsp. each cumin, coriander, fennel, clove, and turmeric,
toasting the whole spices first to release their oils**

1 tsp. cayenne

1 filet striped bass, about 4 lb.

salt and pepper, to taste

extra virgin olive oil

Grind the whole, toasted spices in a grinder or mortar and pestle until fine, and combine with cayenne pepper. Generously season the bass with the spice mix and salt and pepper. Lightly oil the fish, and place it on a hot grill, turning after a couple minutes and flipping (about 6 minutes depending on the thickness).

TOMATOES:

extra virgin olive oil

8 KK's great white tomatoes, sliced into thick wedges

sea salt and black pepper, to taste

Place the tomato wedges on an oiled baking pan, and roast them in a 500-degree oven for 10 minutes or until browned. Salt and pepper to taste, and hold at room temperature until ready to serve.

FRESH YOGURT SAUCE:

1 tbsp. extra virgin olive oil

1 tbsp. garlic, minced

1 tbsp. shallot, minced

1 tbsp. fresh toasted and ground cumin

1 tbsp. mint, chopped

1 tbsp. chives, minced

2 c. fresh goat's milk yogurt

salt and black pepper, to taste

Heat the oil in a small sauté pan over medium-high heat. When hot, add the garlic and shallots, stirring to prevent browning; cook until tender. Remove from the heat, and add the cumin, mint, and chives. Stir to combine, and scrape it all into a small mixing bowl. Add the yogurt, season to taste with salt and black pepper, and chill until ready to serve. Serve family style on a large platter with the fish resting on the roasted tomatoes, or plate them individually for a more formal party.

Scrimshaw

Chef Rosa Ross
Crescent Duck Farm

"Food is memory," states Chef Rosa Ross. This force of nature hails from Macau where she grew up a child of privilege who never forgot the family cooks' multiple visits to the local Hong Kong food markets to get the freshest ingredients.

Now a voice of culinary leadership, Rosa de Carvalho Ross appreciates her culinary cultural heritage, a delicious blend of Chinese, Portuguese, and French cuisines. The memories are so strong, so vivid, that they have consistently fueled her life, with food as the constant road map.

Food has taken Rosa on a career course that includes student, teacher, lecturer, consultant, author, cook, caterer, and restaurateur. Like the Silk Road, hers is an amazing journey that takes her around the globe only to come home—to Long Island.

In 1961, when she married Australian advertising executive Ron Ross, wives just followed their husbands, according to Rosa. When her husband was assigned to work in Milan, his coworker introduced Rosa to his spouse, Marcela Hazan, the Italian cookbook author and teacher hailed as the queen of Italian cooking. They became fast friends, dining together often, and Marcela was soon showing Rosa how to cook typical Italian dishes and acting as her official shopping guide in the local markets.

By the 1970s, after settling in New York, Rosa was working in an advertising agency and also managing the firm's dining room and kitchen, reserved for clients. Encouraged by her colleagues, Rosa also took up teaching cooking classes out of her home kitchen and worked in both jobs for about five years, eventually relinquishing the agency work to focus on the cooking school.

She felt she was on the road to success but determined she needed more credibility as a chef. She joined the International Association of Cooking Teachers, now the International Association of Culinary Professionals (IACP), and served on the professional accreditation committee with Peter Kump, who had an emerging culinary school in Manhattan: the Institute of Culinary Education (ICE). In 1981, Rosa went to work for Kump, taking students and visiting chefs to Chinatown to teach them about the world of fresh Chinese vegetables and herbs.

While continuing to attend IACP annual conferences held across the United States, Rosa had an idea that would further increase her culinary credibility, and her first cookbook, *365 Ways to Cook Chinese*, was published in 1994.

Rosa's introduction to working in restaurants was by way of friend Michelle Jean, who was opening a place to be called Macau in the meatpacking district of Manhattan. Proudly noting that Macau was not only her own birthplace, but also that of true fusion food—as well as recognizing there wasn't another restaurant in the country offering this kind of cuisine—Rosa received a year-long consulting contract to help guide the menu and food operation.

Not long after, Rosa was asked to do a tasting menu for a group of restaurant investors. The food was an unmitigated success, leaving the investors begging *her* to be the executive chef of their newest project. She demurred at first but finally agreed. The restaurant was soon renamed Orient and opened six months later to much acclaim from celebrities and restaurant critics. She had been bitten by the restaurant bug, but the timing was bad.

"After the attacks on the World Trade Center, everything changed," she says. "The investment in downtown and entertainment and restaurants had pretty much dried up. There was no telling when things would turn around."

Rosa was determined to explore other options.

In the 1980s, Rosa and her husband bought their country house in the East End of Long Island. She and her family wanted to enjoy the ambiance of the area and to get away—and use the time to write her books and test recipes. She wanted to spend more time in the North Fork and determined she could open a cooking school there.

In 2003, she seized the opportunity for a restaurant space in Greenport. Rosa's husband, the advertising genius, came up with the name for the restaurant: Scrimshaw. The moniker pays homage to the area's whaling pedigree and the art of scrimshaw. Rosa remarked that at her age, this was going to be an even bigger adventure than anything she'd taken on previously.

Having been on the island for twenty years, Rosa already knew quite a few resources for her food ingredients, including fourth-generation Long Island duck farmer Doug Corwin.

Crescent Duck Farm is an enduring, family-operated labor of love. Up until the 1960s, Long Island was heralded for its duck, with nary a white-tablecloth restaurant across America that didn't list it as a regular item. But after breeding trials and cheaper labor elsewhere produced ducks that arguably began to impact the local Long Island market, the members of Doug's family led the development to produce their own strain of duck and to make their own high-quality duck food. Today, Crescent Farm duck has carved out an enviable niche, dominating the top tier of taste and much in demand by the country's best chefs.

In 2004, after Rosa opened the front door to Scrimshaw, growers and artisanal food producers were knocking on the back door. "We are not a secret, they come to us. Here, it's easy," she says. And for a formidable no-rules chef like Rosa, it is. She's always been a fearless, confident artist. She tries things she's never done before and doesn't even consider failure as an option.

Crescent Farm Duck Breast with Pickled Red Cabbage and Pâté Turnover

Serves 4

At Scrimshaw, we use every part of the ducks we get from Crescent, therefore, for this dish, we use the breasts, reserve the legs and thighs for Duck Confit, which we use in our spring rolls, and turn the livers into our own pâté. We also get wonderful butter puff pastry commercially, but for home use, bought pâté and Pepperidge Farm pastry are good substitutes. Sadly, if you want a really good duck sauce you will have to make the stock—a little tedious but well worth the time.

1 Crescent Farm duck, about 6 lb.

salt and pepper

1 onion, quartered

1 large carrot, peeled and sliced

2–3 celery stalks, whole or cut into 3-inch pieces

1 sprig of thyme

2 bay leaves

1 tbsp. tomato paste

1 c. Duck Sauce

2 c. Pickled Red Cabbage

4 Pâté Turnovers

Remove the breasts from the duck, score the skin, and salt and pepper the meat side. Set aside. Trim the thighs and save them for another use. Remove the liver and gizzards from the duck carcass, and discard. Place the duck carcass in a roasting pan on top of the onion, carrot, celery stalks, thyme, and bay leaves. Roast about 45 minutes in a 350- to 400-degree oven until the meat and vegetables are browned but not burned.

Remove all to a stockpot, then deglaze the pan (always use water to deglaze) and add the liquid to the stockpot. Cover with water, and add 1 tbsp. tomato paste for color. Simmer 4 to 6 hours over low heat until the stock is flavorful. Degrease by using a grease strainer or spoon, or pour off as much fat as you can; return the stock to the pot. Reduce the stock over high heat until about 2 c. remain.

DUCK SAUCE:

duck stock (see above)

6–8 allspice berries

6–8 juniper berries

salt and pepper, to taste

Place the stock in a saucepan and flavor with allspice and juniper berries. Cook until the sauce reduces to a heavy cream consistency. Season with salt and pepper to taste. You should have 1 c. of sauce.

PICKLED CABBAGE:

1 head red cabbage

2 tbsp. vegetable oil

1 red onion, thinly sliced

1 c. dried cranberries or golden raisins

1 c. red wine vinegar

1 c. sugar

1–2 tsp. salt

freshly ground black pepper, to taste

Shred the red cabbage as for slaw. In a deep saucepan, sauté the onion in vegetable oil until wilted, add the cabbage, and stir to cook briefly. Add cranberries or raisins, vinegar, sugar, salt, and black pepper. Reduce the heat to a simmer, and cook until cabbage it is wilted, stirring frequently. Add water, if necessary, to prevent burning. Cool, and store the excess in the refrigerator for another use.

Note: Can be made ahead and will keep 1 month, refrigerated.

PÂTÉ TURNOVERS:

1 sheet puff pastry (Pepperidge Farm works well)

1 egg beaten and mixed with 1 tbsp. cold water

Sliced mousse pâté, about 1/2 inch thick or about 1 heaping tsp. (too much mousse will not allow triangles)

Lay the puff pastry sheet on a clean work surface, and cut into four equal squares. Brush the edges with egg wash. Divide the pâté into four equal parts, and lay on the pastry squares. Turn the pastry square over to form a triangle. Press the edges to seal, and crimp. Brush the tops of turnovers with more of the egg wash. Refrigerate the pastry until firm. Heat the oven to 375 degrees, and bake the pastry turnovers until golden brown (about 15 to 20 minutes). Remove and keep warm.

Note: We make our own pâté, but Les Trois Petits Cochons has an excellent duck mousse pâté, among other brands. Even good homemade chopped chicken liver will work.

To serve duck: In a skillet large enough to hold the duck breasts, cook the duck breasts skin side down over low heat. This will cook off most of the fat. Pour off and save the excess fat for another use. Do not rush this step. When the skin sides are a golden brown, turn and sear the duck breasts on the meat side. Remove the skillet to the oven, and cook until the breasts are rare (about 10 minutes). Remove from oven, and let rest 5 to 10 minutes. Slice to serve.

On each of four plates: Mound 1/2 c. of the Pickled Cabbage, stand a turnover against the cabbage, and arrange the duck slices in front of the turnover. Heat the Duck Sauce and drizzle it over the duck. Serve.

Arroz de Choco (Squid Rice)

Serves 8

In June, when local squid swarm to the waters around our dock at Scrimshaw, I like to prepare this Macau recipe from my childhood. Traditionally, we serve this as a side dish, as an alternative to plain white rice, but with the freshness of the just caught squid, I often enjoy this as a main dish now.

4 medium-sized whole squid
1 piece fresh ginger, about 1 inch long, peeled and minced
1 tbsp. extra virgin olive oil
2 medium yellow onions, peeled and cut into thin wedges
2 c. long grain rice
4 whole cloves
2 bay leaves
6 medium tomatoes, cored and quartered
2 1/2 c. cold water
salt and freshly ground black pepper, to taste

Clean the squid: Cut off tentacles, and set aside. Pull out the beak and entrails, and discard. Peel off the skin. Cut tentacles in half, and cut the body into rings. Combine the squid with the minced ginger in a small bowl, and set aside.

In a medium saucepan, heat the oil over medium heat. Add the onions and cook until soft but not brown (about 5 minutes). Add the rice, cloves, and bay leaves, and cook, stirring, about 30 seconds. Add the tomatoes and water. Increase the heat to medium-high, bring to a boil, and cook about 10 minutes.

Add the squid, season to taste, and stir to blend well. Lower the heat to low, cover, and cook until the liquid is absorbed (about 15 minutes). Let stand for another 5 minutes off the heat to steam. Remove the bay leaves, and serve.

Vegetable Blender Soup

Serves 4–6

This is a favorite of my family—it is soothing when you are feeling under the weather and not up to eating too much. One can usually harvest the ingredients from what you have in your vegetable bin, and each time, depending on your vegetable mix, it tastes a little different. When using garden fresh produce from the farmstands, it can be exceptional.

1–2 large potatoes, peeled and cut into chunks
4 stalks celery, cut up
4 medium-sized carrots, peeled and sliced
4–6 green leaves, such as cabbage or lettuce or even a
 handful of spinach
2 ripe tomatoes, or 4–6 plum tomatoes, quartered
handful of parsley
1–2 parsnips or turnips, peeled and cut into chunks (optional)
2–4 tbsp. butter
salt and pepper, to taste

In a saucepan, combine all the vegetables with just enough water to barely cover. Add a good chunk of butter and salt and pepper to taste. Cook until the vegetables are tender.

With a slotted spoon remove the vegetables to the jar of a blender or a food processor. Process to a smooth purée. Add the water in which the vegetables have been cooked. Process to blend. Return the mixture to the pot, add enough water or milk to make a smooth soup. Add a little more butter if desired. Season to taste and serve.

Vine Street Café

Chefs Terry and Lisa Harwood
Sylvester Manor Farm

Born in East Tennessee on the family's beloved "Homestead," Chef Terry Harwood lived almost a double life after his parents' divorce, spending the school year with his mother in the urban projects and living the rural, homegrown life in the summer with his father.

Built in the 1920s, the Homestead is the cornerstone of a proud farming community. In years past, the harvest was all handpicked by the family and brought to the local cooperative, "where food, tools, and other necessities were bartered, and the men exchanged news while whittling cedar posts and chewing tobacco," Terry explains.

At the community's lone restaurant, Season's Goodness, one could flirt with such "exotic" menu items as hamburgers and French fries, Terry recalls affectionately. Becoming a chef was a never-considered flight of fantasy. Rather, his early aspiration was to be a lawyer, so Terry enrolled at the University of Tennessee as a political science major. To help pay for expenses, Terry took his first restaurant job as a pizza cook and dishwasher, then moved to the fine dining of Perry's Seafood restaurant, which altered his ambitions.

Ali, a Zen-like Moroccan chef at Perry's who was an alchemist of sorts, taught him about spices. To Terry, the world was suddenly exotic and expansive, then Perry's chef Jim Rechard urged Terry to quit waiting tables and become a chef. Determined to get his cooking credentials from the school of experience, Terry started his food pilgrimage in Chicago, not too far from home.

Someone recommended he begin his housing search in Lincoln Park, and while on a site inspection of the neighborhood that first day, he saw a help wanted posting in the window of Italian restaurant Bella Vista. His intention was to wait tables and make some money to establish his new life, but by the end of his interview, Terry was in prep clothes.

Bella Vista's Chef Geoff Felsenthal helped Terry secure a second, part-time stagier position in the impossible-to-get-into Charlie Trotter kitchen. On his rare time off from Bella Vista's, Terry worked gratis at Trotter's—just for the unmatched experience.

Terry's New York break came when he was recruited to Fish 'N' Eddy's and then to Harbour Lights, where he made frequent use of the Fulton Fish Market in lower Manhattan before being hired by Michael Romano, executive chef of Union Square Café. It was here, at New York's perennial top-tier restaurant, that Terry learned how to work the greenmarkets. "We started conversations with the farmers—many of whom I now use today—making that connection from farm to table."

Union Square Café is also where he met his wife, Lisa, who came to work as the new pastry chef.

Smitten by the farm-fresh food, Terry took an offer from Tracy Jardin to help open her namesake Jardiniere San Francisco restaurant, but all too soon, he missed Manhattan—and Lisa. Back in Gotham, Terry and Lisa were hired to run the food operations at four of Andre Balzac's posh hotels, with home base for the winter in a bungalow at the storied Hotel Chateau Marmot in LA and summers spent on Shelter Island at the Sunset Beach Bistro by the Sea restaurant.

It was a fantasy life to be sure, but after four years it was time for a change. Lisa and Terry wanted to pursue their own country island restaurant and raise a family. They searched for a place they could buy on Shelter Island and found a shack with "bones" and history. After remodeling every square inch of the place, they opened the Vine Street Café's doors in 2002.

Sourcing local food on Shelter Island will always be a challenge, since everything needs to be ferried in. Over time, his relationships with growers and suppliers have allowed Terry to enjoy deliveries two to three times a week, but it takes a lot of meticulous planning and oversight.

Terry and Lisa work so closely with Bennett Konesni at Sylvester Manor Farm that they even gave him their chickens when it was deemed in the birds' best interest to relocate from the restaurant at Vine Street.

Bennett operates the 243-acre Sylvester Manor, a colonial family heritage granted by royal charter dating from 1652. Under Bennett's stewardship, the working farm operates as a nonprofit educational cultural landscape.

Creek Iverson, head farmer who works most directly with the Harwoods, was an environmental sciences teacher who easily transitioned to farming. He explains that part of the farm's mission is to satisfy the people of Shelter Island with a sustainable food supply. The Manor Farm Stand is open twenty-four hours a day where farmers put fresh produce in the cooler and customers select from the just-picked food and leave money in an honesty box.

Chefs at local restaurants make up one of four key audiences for the Manor. "They are clamoring for stuff we grow," says Creek proudly.

The Vine Street menu changes once a week, and reinforcing the homegrown narrative, Terry says that up to 80 percent is sourced locally or regionally with almost every item tagged with the food's provenance. Looking ahead, Terry and Lisa hope to continue just what they are doing but do more of it, possibly opening more restaurants and developing a line of local homegrown take-home items.

One thing is for sure, Terry knows how to work with a sustainable "garden-to-plate" restaurant to make it an enduring success.

Grilled Montauk Swordfish with Picatta-Style Sauce and Fresh Baby Spinach

Serves 4

First, make sure you have a hot grill. . . . When I grill at home I make sure the lid is closed at all times to ensure high heat. I will also throw a slice of wet oak or a small pan of wood chips in the corner to provide a little smoke with the gas grill.

4 swordfish steaks, thick and center cut, about 7–8 oz. each
extra virgin olive oil
sea salt and black pepper
1 c. Brown Butter Vinaigrette
2 tbsp. parsley
6 yellow pears or cherry tomatoes, fresh, chopped and
    quartered lengthwise
6 red pears or cherry tomatoes, quartered lengthwise
1 tbsp. small capers, rinsed
baby spinach, for garnish
1 lemon, sliced for garnish

Rub the swordfish lightly with extra virgin olive oil, and sprinkle with sea salt and black pepper. Open the grill, brush it clean, wipe it with oil, and close the lid for 1 minute.

With tongs at the ready, open the lid and place the fish on the grill at a 10 o'clock position. Close the lid immediately, and wait 2 to 3 minutes. Open the lid, and move your fish from the ten o'clock position to a two o'clock position, creating an X mark on the grilled side. Close the lid, and wait another 2 to 3 minutes. Open the lid, and turn the fish over. Repeat the marking process on the unmarked side. Depending on the thickness of the fish, the cooking time should be 6 to 10 minutes. If the fish is large and flat, use a spatula instead of a pair of tongs.

Note: I like my swordfish cooked medium to medium well but not well done. When you take your swordfish off the grill, immediately put the sauce together.

For the sauce: Mix your Brown Butter Vinaigrette, parsley, quartered yellow and red tomatoes, capers, and a little sea salt and pepper in a small bowl.

For plating: Slice a handful of baby spinach into wide ribbons. Divide the spinach onto 4 plates, and place a piece of swordfish on each. Spoon the sauce over the fish, dividing the tomatoes evenly between the 4 swordfish steaks. Add lemon slices for garnish.

Variation: Mix thinly sliced artichoke hearts (frozen will work) into the sauce.

BROWN BUTTER VINAIGRETTE:
1/2 lb. butter, organic
2 each lemons, zest one, juice both
1 tbsp. Dijon mustard
2 tbsp. champagne vinegar
1/2 c. extra virgin olive oil
1/4 tsp. black pepper
1/2 tsp. sea salt

There are elements of danger with this recipe, so be careful when dealing with hot butter. In a 2-qt. stainless-steel sauce pot, add the butter, place on high heat, and bring to a hard sizzle. This can be a little scary and a little dangerous, so do not attempt this recipe unless you are comfortable. Let the butter sizzle hard until you think it starts turning brown. When it starts to turn brown, turn off the heat and let the butter cool down at the back of the stove top (about 15 minutes).

After 15 minutes the butter will still be hot but workable. Add all your ingredients, and blend with an immersion hand blender until somewhat emulsified. This sauce will keep for a couple of weeks in the refrigerator. Before using, make sure it's malleable and loose. Because of the butter, chilling it makes it hard, so you will have to warm it up a little; a few seconds in the microwave should do it. Toss with parsley and capers for a "picatta" style sauce for grilled fish. Get creative and add fresh shallots or tomatoes and herbs as a sauce for grilled chicken. A little goes a long way.

Sticky Toffee Pudding

with Toasted Almond Brittle

From Pastry Chef Lisa Harwood

Serves 8–10

STICKY TOFFEE PUDDING:

3/4 c. dates, chopped and pitted

1 c. boiling water

1/4 c. brewed coffee (French roast or full bodied)

1 tsp. baking soda

4 tbsp. unsalted butter (room temperature)

3/4 c. sugar

1 large egg (room temperature)

1 tsp. vanilla extract

1 c. plus 1 tbsp. all-purpose flour

pinch salt

1 tsp. baking powder

1/4 c. walnuts, chopped and lightly toasted

1/4 c. bittersweet chocolate, roughly chopped

3/4 c. pitted dates, chopped

Preheat a convection oven to 325 degrees or a conventional oven to 350 degrees. Lightly grease a 9x5-inch ceramic loaf pan. Measure all the ingredients. Sift together the flour, baking powder, and salt in a bowl, then add the chopped chocolate and walnuts. In a separate bowl, place the chopped dates and coffee, baking soda, and boiling water. Set aside.

In an electric mixer fitted with a paddle attachment, cream the butter and sugar until light and fluffy. Add the egg and vanilla, and beat until blended. With the mixer on low, add the flour mixture to the batter and mix until just combined. Pour the dates and coffee into the batter, and mix until just combined. Scrape down sides of the bowl with a spatula, and stir to make sure the batter is evenly mixed. Pour batter into the loaf pan (previously greased). Bake until "pudding" is set and a cake tester (toothpick) comes out clean. It will look like a cake when it is finished.

TOFFEE SAUCE:

8 tbsp. unsalted butter

1/2 c. heavy cream

1 c. packed dark brown sugar

pinch salt

Place all of the ingredients in a stainless-steel saucepan. Slowly bring to a boil, stirring constantly with a wooden spoon. Boil gently over medium to low heat until the sauce has thickened (about 10 minutes). Be careful not to overcook the sauce; it should have the consistency of a warm caramel sauce.

TOASTED ALMOND BRITTLE:

1 1/3 c. water

4 c. sugar

3/4 c. corn syrup

2 sticks (16 tbsp.) sweet organic or unsalted butter

1/2 tsp. salt

1/2 tsp. baking soda

4 c. toasted sliced almonds

To make the caramel, combine the water, sugar, corn syrup, butter, and salt in a stainless-steel pot. Cook without stirring until mixture becomes a light-colored caramel. Turn the stove off, and quickly yet carefully stir in the baking soda. Add nuts. Turn the mixture out onto a silpat/silicone mat or baking sheet, and spread evenly with the back of a wooden spoon. Move quickly and carefully. Caramel cools quickly, making it difficult to spread while remaining seriously hot to the touch.

To serve: Remove the Toffee Pudding from the baking pan, and place on a small sheet pan. Pour half the Toffee Sauce over the cake, and place under the broiler until the sauce starts to bubble. Take the cake out of the oven, and place on a serving dish. Pour the remaining half of the sauce over the cake. Rough chop the Toasted Almond Brittle and sprinkle it over the cake. The Sticky Toffee Pudding can be served with your favorite ice cream or fresh whipped cream.

Sticky Toffee Pudding
with Toasted Almond Brittle

18 Bay

Chefs Adam Kopels and Elizabeth Ronzetti
Sang Lee Farms

Shelter Island chefs Elizabeth Ronzetti and Adam Kopels characterize 18 Bay as an "inspired seafood restaurant" because it emulates the great seafood restaurants on the Ligurian coast (in Italy), which won't open when stormy weather threatens or the catch of the day is nonexistent. Once you taste even a sampling of the chefs' culinary work, you won't care what hours they choose to keep. You won't care about anything more than their food.

A shared dedication to fresh, local food prepared in simple ways is what brought Elizabeth and Adam together. In 2004, Long Island native Elizabeth had just finished culinary school and was looking for a place to do her three-hundred-hour externship. At that time and in that part of Long Island, she says, there weren't many places cooking the way she wanted to cook. Then she happened upon a Huntington restaurant where Adam was the chef. She perused his menu offerings from the posting next to the door and, finding the recipes appealing, walked in and asked, "Do you guys need help?"

Soon, she was wowing Adam, the staff, and the customers with menu items like lemon-scented-ricotta-stuffed zucchini blossoms and homemade black-ink tagliolini pasta made from locally caught squid.

Adam, who had ten years of formal restaurant training and had worked under such well-known chefs as Tom Collicheo and Mario Batali, immediately recognized that Elizabeth understood food. Seeing her passion, he begged her to stay on as his sous chef after her externship.

She promptly turned him down. She'd never doubted she would one day own a restaurant, and she'd found the perfect little space in Bayville for exactly the kind of restaurant she wanted. So he quit his job to work for her instead.

Theirs was not yet a romantic partnering (that would come later), but Adam says that when he cooked and planned menus with Elizabeth, their talents flowed together naturally, and they both intuitively recognized their good fortune.

Adam had learned to appreciate homegrown foods while working at Babbo Ristorante e Enoteca, a restaurant co-owned by Mario Batali, who was becoming known as a celebrity chef on the brand-new Food Network. Cooks for any of Batali's restaurants were expected to utilize local farmers' markets. The cooks had to be at the market first thing in the morning, buy their products, and then be creative with ingredients they'd procured.

In 2001, Adam moved to San Francisco, but within weeks, he returned home to New York. He missed his native terroir. Taking a job at a small restaurant near Huntington, Long Island, he'd decided that the setting for his next life chapter would be the reed grass and dunes of the South Fork when Elizabeth walked into his restaurant.

It was a dream come true when Elizabeth and Adam opened 18 Bay in 2005. Their delicious, exciting food quickly made the restaurant a jewel that customers couldn't wait to recommend. It didn't

hurt the restaurant's burgeoning popularity when they garnered a top review in the *New York Times*. They had had no clue Joanne Starkey, the *Times* Long Island restaurant critic, had even dined at 18 Bay until a *Times* photographer came in to take photos to run with the review. When it appeared on July 2, 2006, the restaurant had been open only a little over a year. The two chefs returned to 18 Bay after the Fourth of July weekend to field more than 450 calls for reservations in their sixteen-seat restaurant!

Today, the chefs shop their local markets May through November, load up their car till it can't possibly fit another leek or lettuce head, and go to the kitchen to cook up their creations.

Harking back to her childhood, when her family developed relationships with local farmers and baymen by simply asking, "Can I get my eggs from you?" or "Will you supply us with scallops or lobster?" Elizabeth has developed relationships with the local producers to get fresh, pure ingredients for 18 Bay. The farmers and fisherman now call Elizabeth and Adam's mobile phones when something comes in that the chefs want.

Adam and Elizabeth's garden inspiration is Sang Lee Farms, located not far from 18 Bay on Shelter Island where the restaurant relocated in 2011. Run by a third-generation farming family, Sang Lee Farms is a well-respected and recognized brand name, synonymous with organic, delicious produce and present at most of the farmers' markets in the New York City area. Sang Lee Farms boasts: "The moderate climate, offered by the location between the Long Island Sound and Peconic Bay, allows an extended growing season that capitalizes on the fertile, well-drained, sandy loam soils of eastern Long Island." They proudly provide certified organic "Fresh-Lee-Cut" products, growing more than one hundred varieties of specialty vegetables, heirloom tomatoes, baby greens, mesclun, herbs, and specialty Asian greens.

"We live in the most important food area in the world," the chefs say, adding that they feel privileged to showcase the spectrum of local Long Island food. "We'll take you to Southhold, and you can stand in ankle deep water on Peconic Bay. And at your feet, there will be scallops and oysters and sea rockets on the sandy South Shore. We dare you to say there's any more beautiful place in the world."

Immaculata's Stuffed Peppers

Serves 4 as an entrée

PEPPERS:

4 large red bell peppers

Slice off the top of the peppers; set aside the tops. Remove the seeds from the inside of the peppers. Thinly slice off the bottom of peppers without cutting all the way through. (This will allow peppers to stand upright while you're filling them.)

SAUCE:

1/2 large sweet onion, chopped

5 tbsp. olive oil

2 cloves garlic, sliced

12–15 ripe plum tomatoes, peeled, seeded, and chopped,
**   or 1 (28 oz.) can San Marzano Italian peeled plum tomatoes**

salt and pepper

1 fresh bay leaf

handful fresh basil

4 sprigs fresh oregano

On low heat, sauté the chopped onion in olive oil until it is translucent. Add the sliced garlic, and sauté until fragrant; do not brown. Add tomatoes, salt and pepper, bay leaf, basil, and oregano. Simmer gently while preparing stuffing.

STUFFING:

8 large eggs

4 tbsp. Italian parsley, chopped

4 tbsp. extra virgin olive oil

salt and pepper, to taste

1 c. Parmesan cheese, grated

1/2 c. fresh bread crumbs

In medium bowl, beat the eggs, parsley, oil, and salt and pepper until well blended. Add the cheese and bread crumbs until well incorporated. The stuffing should be fairly thick.

Assembling and cooking: Preheat the oven to 350 degrees. Stand the peppers upright. Spoon the stuffing into the peppers, filling them three-quarters full. Replace the pepper tops. Ladle half the tomato sauce into a baking dish. Place the peppers, standing upright, into baking pan, and ladle the remaining sauce over the peppers. Cover the peppers with foil, and bake 50 to 60 minutes until the peppers are tender and the stuffing is set. Allow the peppers to rest for 5 to 10 minutes. Serve the peppers sliced with sauce spooned over; garnish with fresh parsley and basil.

Barbecue Striped Bass Fin

Serves 2

FIN VINAIGRETTE:

1 c. balsamic vinegar

3 jalapeños or other fresh chilies, chopped with
**   seeds included**

juice of 1 lime

1/4 c. honey

1/2 tsp. salt

1/2 c. olive oil

In a food processor, combine the balsamic, chilies, lime juice, honey, and salt. Process until fully incorporated. Stream the oil through the top of the food processor to emulsify. Set aside in a bowl.

FISH:

1/2 of a bass pectoral (ask your fishmonger to clean and cut
**   the fish, and secure the fish pectoral with the skin on)**
olive oil to coat
salt and pepper

You will need a very hot grill and a brush to mop the fin. Pat the fish dry with a paper towel, and brush liberally with olive oil to keep it from sticking to the grill. Season on all sides with salt and pepper.

Place the fin, skin side down, on the hottest spot on the grill. Mop the top with vinaigrette. Check the fin after a few minutes. If it doesn't lift off the grill easily, don't move it. Continue to mop the fin with vinaigrette. When it can lift off the grill (usually after about 5 to 7 minutes), mop one more time and then flip it, so it's skin side up. Mop the skin side and continue cooking until the meat starts to pull away from the collarbone. Mop the top one more time, and flip the fin over again to resear the top.

Remove from the grill to a plate. Serve with an herb garden salad dressed with just a little lemon juice and olive oil. We like whole herbs, thin-sliced radishes, purslane, and foraged sea rocket for a contributory salinity.

Black Bow-Tie Pasta
with Local Squid and Guy Lok

Serves 4 as an appetizer, 2 as an entrée

You will need a round single ravioli cutter, preferably fluted.

PASTA:

2 c. all-purpose flour
1 tbsp. semolina (or Durham flour), plus more for dusting
2 eggs
pinch of salt
1/2 tsp. olive oil
contents of the ink sacs from the squid (squid ink is also available from your fishmonger)

Mix the flour with the semolina. Make a well with the flour, and break eggs into the well. Beat the eggs with a fork, and mix in the salt, olive oil, and squid ink squeezed from the ink sacs. Gradually work in the flour and bring all together into a ball. Knead the ball for about 5 minutes, or until it feels smooth and springs back slowly when pressed with your thumb. Cover with plastic wrap, and let rest for at least 20 minutes.

Divide the dough in half, and roll it out for cutting. Cut out discs with the ravioli cutter. Make bow ties by folding the discs in half and holding the dough between the thumb and forefinger with both hands, pressing the dough together 1/8 inch from the seam; repeat, folding back and forth like an accordion to make even pleats with the dough. Pinch in the center, and place on a sheet tray, liberally dusted with semolina, to dry.

Prepare a large pot of boiling salted water. Cook the pasta in the boiling water for 2 minutes. Remove from the water, and drain.

FOR THE DISH:

2 lb. fresh whole, medium-sized squid
1 lb. guy lok (Chinese broccoli), broccoli rabe, or any young summer greens
1 tbsp. olive oil
2 garlic cloves, sliced thin
1/4 tsp. crushed red pepper

Clean the squid by pulling the tentacles from the body and removing the contents of the body or tube. Reserve the silvery black ink sacs for the pasta. Remove the beaks from the tentacles, cut the tubes into 1-inch rings, and set aside the beaks and the tubes.

Rough chop the greens, and sauté in a large sauté pan with the olive oil, garlic, and red pepper. When the greens are wilted, add a ladleful of pasta water to the pan to steam the greens.

Add the cooked, drained pasta to the pan with greens. Bring to a boil, and add the squid. Cook for just about 2 minutes to cook the squid through gently. Serve immediately.

The North Shore

Long Island's northern coastline has, for generations, been considered the region's most opulent and wealthiest area, earning its nickname of the "Gold Coast." Today, the heritage farms and diverse ethnic population settled here have inspired a cornucopia of greenmarkets and authentic restaurants with distinctive cuisines from Italian to French to Greek to Eastern European.

Mitch & Toni's American Bistro

Chef Mitchell SuDock

The Rottkamp Farm

Mitchell SuDock's resume is impressive. A top-of-the-class graduate of the Culinary Institute of America (CIA) in Hyde Park, New York, he put his education to work during an externship at the famous Russian Tea Room in Manhattan. After that experience, he knew he wanted to work for a restaurant that respected food.

"The first and only job I wanted was at Gotham Bar & Grill," he says.

As he found when he succeeded in landing that job, Gotham Bar & Grill was very busy and big, and the kitchen generated an undercurrent of high-intensity, focused work. During his time there, he worked a lot of the kitchen's stations, assisting sous chef Bill Telepan and eventually becoming his right-hand man.

In addition to giving Mitchell a mentor and valuable career experience, Gotham also introduced him to what would become his future passion: cooking with fresh, locally harvested food. Instead of getting its produce from wholesalers, like most New York City restaurants did in the 1990s, the Gotham chefs shopped at Union Square Greenmarket, a huge farmers' market just two blocks away from the restaurant. When Mitchell worked there, the sous chef called in orders to the farmers on Mondays, and the produce was picked on Tuesdays. On Wednesdays, the chefs would meet with the farmers to talk about weather and its effects on the produce, what was in season, and what was looking especially good.

Mitchell's farm-to-table education continued at Ansonia, the Upper West Side restaurant he helped Telepan open in 1994, but getting fresh food from Union Square was more of a challenge there than it had been at Gotham. Every day the Greenmarket was open, the chefs would load up three to four cabs with produce, hauling as much as they could.

Mitchell says being exposed to fresh-from-the-farm ingredients early in his restaurant career helped him establish his own cooking philosophy so that in 2004, when he opened Bistro M in what was formerly a Long Island candy store, he knew food from local producers would be the basis for his menus.

When Mitchell was growing up on Long Island, his family had a modest ornamental vegetable garden in their yard, along with wild mint and a spot for growing basil. Today, at his successful Mitch & Toni's American Bistro restaurant, Mitchell grows the same plants for garnishes. His brother and sister-in-law bring him fresh fruits and vegetables from their garden's end-of-summer surplus, as does one of Mitchell's neighbors. And the restaurant manager has a neighbor who simply leaves foodstuffs on their doorstep. The bounty of Long Island is such that it turns the locals into botanical Robin Hoods.

Mitchell is happy to once again be close to the Long Island farms he knew growing up, including the Rottkamp Farm, located a few miles from his restaurant. The Rottkamps are part of a Long Island farming dynasty that goes back generations. Today, these two

Rottkamp farmers are brothers, married to two French sisters, Anne Marie and Michelle, who help manage the 150-acre farm along with their husbands. Mitchell rediscovered the Rottkamp Farm when setting out to establish his farm resources for Bistro M.

"I grew up on a Long Island street where my family's backyard bordered the Rottkamp Farm and Rottkamp Lane," Mitchell says. "My friends and I would sneak onto the farm and have vegetable fights before the farmers would chase us off."

Food purveyors continually offer to get him anything at any time of year, but Mitchell says cooking with out-of-season or out-of-state food is not what he wants to do. "Why would I want to get peaches from Ohio or Ojai? . . . We already lost one generation to Betty Crocker," he says with restrained judgment.

Mitchell sometimes thinks of himself as a teacher for the restaurant's staff and customers, and he finds that customers are always eager to learn more about what they are eating. Mitchell leaves the kitchen most nights to greet his guests, urging them to try this or that. Sometimes customers are ambivalent about eating something they haven't had before, preferring the familiar or safe, so he sends out things for them to try. The food's quality and extraordinary taste have earned him not only followers, but also glowing, three-star reviews from the *New York Times*, *Newsday*, and Zagat.

Mitchell is so keen to expose more people to good food that he has produced a series of successful tasting events. He creates new menus every week, with daily additions in each of the categories, based on market conditions. Out of respect for their work and contributions to the restaurant's success, he includes the names of local farmers and fishermen on the menu.

The biggest changes he sees coming in the world of Long Island food are "how [regular] things get redefined," which suggests that Mitchell SuDock is already looking at things in a new way, using the limitless local possibilities waiting to be rediscovered.

Pistachio-Crusted Halibut with Asparagus, Fava Beans, Oyster Mushrooms, and Lemon Beurre Blanc

Serves 4

PISTACHIO CRUST:

    1/2 c. pistachios, ground
    1/2 c. fresh bread crumbs
    1/4 lb. butter, softened
    1/2 tsp. lemon juice
    salt and white pepper, to taste

Place all the ingredients in a food processor, and purée until smooth. Place a piece of wax paper on the back of a baking sheet. Spread the mixture 1/4 inch thick, and place the sheet in the freezer; chill 2 hours. Cut the crust into four equal portions (or the same size as the fish).

LEMON BEURRE BLANC:

    4 tbsp. white wine
    2 tbsp. lemon juice, freshly squeezed
    1 tsp. heavy cream
    1/2 c. (1 stick) sweet butter, diced into 1/4-inch cubes
    salt and pepper, to taste

Place the white wine and lemon juice in a nonreactive pot, and reduce to almost dry. Add the cream, swirl once, and add the butter over moderate heat while swirling the pan. *Do not boil.* Season with salt and pepper. Set aside in a warm but not hot place.

HALIBUT ASSEMBLY:

    4 halibut filets, 6 oz. each
    salt and pepper, to taste
    Lemon Beurre Blanc
    16 asparagus spears, blanched
    1/2 c. fava beans, cooked
    1 c. oyster mushrooms, cooked
    water
    butter
    salt and pepper
    Pistachio Crust

Preheat the oven to 400 degrees. Season the fish with salt and pepper. Place the halibut filets, topped with Lemon Beurre Blanc, in a nonstick sauté pan or on a sheet tray sprayed with nonstick cooking spray. Place the fish in the oven, and cook 12 to 15 minutes until a small knife inserted into the middle of the fish comes out hot.

Meanwhile, heat the asparagus, fava beans, and mushrooms in a pan with a little water, butter, salt, and pepper for approximately 2 minutes. Place an equal amount of vegetables on each plate.

Remove the fish from the oven, and using a spatula, place a piece of fish on top of the vegetables. Sauce the plate with about 3 tbsp. Lemon Beurre Blanc and enjoy.

Serving Suggestions: Serve with polenta or steamed potatoes. Substitute spring vegetables like peas, carrots, or spring onions.

Grilled Octopus with Panzanella Salad

Serves 4

GRILLED OCTOPUS:

- **2 tbsp. olive oil**
- **2 carrots, roughly chopped**
- **2 stalks celery, roughly chopped**
- **1 onion, roughly chopped**
- **6 cloves garlic, minced**
- **1/2 head fennel, roughly chopped**
- **3–4 sprigs fresh thyme and/or oregano**
- **1 tbsp. black peppercorns**
- **1 piece tenderized octopus, 2–4 lb.**
- **3 c. white wine**
- **2 qt. water**
- **1/4 c. white wine vinegar**
- **kosher salt as needed**

Heat the oil in a 12 qt. stockpot. Add the vegetables, and cook on moderate heat 5 minutes, stirring often. Add the thyme, oregano, and peppercorns, and cook 2 minutes more. Add the octopus, liquids, and salt, and bring to a boil over high heat. Once boiling, reduce heat to a simmer, and place one to two plates on top of the octopus to weight it down and keep it submerged. Cook the octopus 1 to 1 1/2 hours, until tender. *Note:* To determine doneness, remove the octopus from the pot and taste a small piece by cutting into it at the base (head) where all the tentacles come together.

When the octopus is done, remove it from the liquid. When the octopus is cool enough to handle, cut each tentacle away from the base by cutting into the base on each side of the tentacles. You will have eight pieces. (The octopus may be cooked up to 2 days ahead of time and refrigerated.) You may remove any skin that is falling off. Lightly oil and season the octopus with salt and pepper, and grill on moderate heat until it is warm and has grill marks.

PANZANELLA SALAD VINAIGRETTE:

- **1/2 c. red wine vinegar**
- **1 c. tomato water (made from puréeing tomatoes and draining them overnight through a coffee filter)**
- **1/2 c. extra virgin olive oil**
- **salt and pepper, to taste**

Combine all ingredients.

PANZANELLA SALAD:

- **2 c. toasted sourdough-bread croutons**
- **Panzanella Salad Vinaigrette**
- **salt and pepper, to taste**
- **2 c. diced tomatoes (heirlooms, if available)**
- **1 c. cherry tomatoes**
- **1/2 c. basil chiffonade**
- **1/2 c. roasted peppers, julienned**
- **1/4 c. sliced red onion**
- **2 tbsp. capers**

Mix together the croutons and a generous amount of Panzanella Salad Vinaigrette, salt, and pepper. Let stand 5 minutes for bread to soak up liquid. Add the rest of the ingredients, and toss with some more vinaigrette until well coated. Season with more salt and pepper. Divide salad among four plates, place Grilled Octopus on top of salad, and drizzle any remaining vinaigrette around the plate.

Spiced Roasted Venison Loin with Squash Spaetzle, Cauliflower-Horseradish Mash, and Huckleberries

Serves 4

SQUASH SPAETZLE:

2 1/3 c. flour

1/2 tsp. nutmeg

1/2 tsp. cinnamon

1 tsp. salt

2 eggs

4 egg yolks

1 c. butternut squash purée, drained

1/2–3/4 c. milk

canola oil

whole butter, as needed

salt and white pepper, to season

Place a large pot of salted water on the stove and bring it to a boil.

Combine the flour, nutmeg, cinnamon, and salt. In a separate bowl, mix well the eggs, yolks, squash purée, and *half* of the milk.

Add the wet mixture to the dry ingredients, and mix well with a large spoon. The mixture should be somewhat elastic. If it is too tough, add more milk, a drop at a time. If it is too loose, add a bit of flour at a time until the mixture breaks apart when mixed with a spoon.

Load a spaetzle press three-quarters full. Squeeze the mixture in one continuous stream into the boiling water. Let all the dough rise to the surface and the water return to a boil. Remove the spaetzle, and shock it in an ice bath. Once all the spaetzle is blanched, drain it, oil it with canola oil, and drain it again very well. Melt 3 tbsp. butter in a sauté pan over medium heat. Once the butter starts to foam, add the spaetzle. Cook until golden brown on one side, flip like a pancake, and brown the other side. Season with salt and white pepper.

CAULIFLOWER MASH:

1 head cauliflower, roughly chopped

4 c. milk (approximately)

1 1/2 c. water (approximately)

2 tbsp. salt

1/8 tsp. ground white pepper

1/8 tsp. nutmeg, freshly grated

1 Yukon gold potato (about 1/4 the amount of the cauliflower)

fresh horseradish, finely grated

splash of white wine vinegar

salt and pepper, to season

Chop the cauliflower, place it in a pot, and cover it with milk and water. (Add more water if needed.) Add salt, pepper, and nutmeg. Bring to a boil, reduce to a simmer, and cook until tender. Meanwhile, boil the potato.

In a small bowl, combine the horseradish and vinegar, and season with salt to taste. Combine the cauliflower, potato, and horseradish mixture, and season with salt and pepper. If needed, adjust the seasoning using the reserved cooking liquid. The final mixture should be stiff enough to hold up to a quenelle on the plate.

HUCKLEBERRIES:

1 lb. fresh or frozen huckleberries

1/2 c. red wine vinegar

1 c. sugar

8 oz. fresh huckleberries

Combine fresh or frozen huckleberries with the vinegar and the sugar; bring to a boil and simmer until reduced by half. Remove from the stove, purée in a blender, and strain through a fine chinois. Return the strained purée to the pot, add the second 8 oz. of berries, return to a boil, and *immediately* remove from the stove. Pour into a saucepan, and cool.

SPICE MIX FOR VENISON:

1 tbsp. whole allspice

4 tbsp. whole coriander seed

1 tsp. whole cumin

2 tbsp. whole juniper

2 tsp. black peppercorns

Toast and grind all ingredients, and shake onto the meat after plating.

VENISON SAUCE:

venison scraps, as needed

2 shallots, sliced

1 clove garlic, sliced

1 c. orange juice

1/2 c. sherry vinegar

1 qt. venison or veal stock

1 c. water

Sear the venison over high heat until brown. Add the shallots and garlic, and cook until the vegetables are soft. Deglaze with orange juice and sherry vinegar, and reduce to sec (meaning until it is dry) about 5 minutes over medium heat. Add stock and water, and simmer until proper taste and consistency is achieved.

To plate: Let the cooked venison rest 5 minutes to redistribute juices and prevent bleeding. Put a spoonful of cauliflower mash on the plate at 12 o'clock, then a spoonful of spaetzle at 6 o'clock. Slice the venison and lay it in the middle of the plate, covering half the cauliflower and half the spaetzle. Drizzle the huckleberries around everything, and spoon a small amount of sauce on the plate.

CoolFish Grille & Wine Bar

Chef Tom Schaudel

Paumanok Vineyards

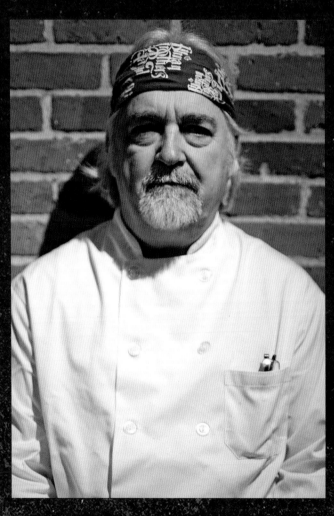

Chef Tom Schaudel is a food lover you can't admonish for "playing with his food." An exuberant chef, Tom grew up in Carle Place, Long Island. His Swiss grandmother lived with the family, passing on the culinary lessons acquired during her work as a cook in Swiss hotels.

Tom started working in restaurants as a dishwasher, lying about his age in order to get the necessary working papers, all so he could make money, he says, to buy a girlfriend a bracelet. What he found was a party.

"It was a boat-load of fun," says Tom, laughing. "I knew I'd discovered my Plan B, in case I didn't make it as a musician," he recalls, grinning at the serendipity.

That Plan B career option has allowed Tom to spend over forty years as a professional chef, launching and managing more than fourteen restaurants. Today, Tom oversees a portfolio of food services in his restaurant and consulting business and is a popular radio show host and TV personality on the Food Channel. He is more like the rock star he once aspired to be, with local press claiming Tom "rules Long Island's restaurant scene." And he is the only Long Island chef to be named to the Long Island Hall of Fame by the Long Island Dining Alliance (LIDA).

Tom's family moved from Flushing Queens to be in the country, and he fondly remembers the ruralness of his childhood home in Carle Place. He vibrantly tells about the Huck Finn–like existence he enjoyed every summer at his Aunt Pearl's—foraging fresh huckleberries in the Bayville woods, fishing for glimmering silver-striped bass, clamming on the beach.

Taste drove his culinary passions then, and it does now.

Nurturing and developing local food resources for the restaurants happened slowly, he notes, as many long-term relationships do. It wasn't work. It was more romance. And this Long Island native knew whom to talk to. "It's like Disneyland for food out here," he pronounces with glee. In a rapid fire riff, he names a top ten list of his food partners, all longtime food craftspeople who provide fresh, tasty, sustainable food for Long Island.

Metaphorically, he describes having to "hack a path" to help lead the local food evolution on the road to acceptance. But while it is a tough challenge to consistently provide local comestibles, especially during winter on Long Island, it can be done with great flavor and creativity, Tom maintains. He also points to Mother Nature smiling on Long Island, noting the variety of fish that make this paradise their home too, such as the Peconic Bay's tasty seasonal scallops and oysters. Discovering sources as disparate as the man himself fuels Tom's culinary inspiration.

To help spark his culinary creative juices, he takes one or two international food trips a year. He's even taught cooking in China. To satiate the intermediate food temptations, he'll take a one- or two-day trip to food emporiums in Philadelphia or Chicago. "My curiosity about

Grant Achatz's Alinia or Charlie Trotter on one end of the scale to the small, out of the way places is always driving my quest and impacting my cooking," says Tom.

He claims he's eaten out every night since 1967. "I also read more than half a dozen cooking magazines a month," and he describes how he consistently refers to his ever-expanding cookbook library of around six hundred tomes. Tom's passion for food and cooking and telling restaurant stories led him to make room in his schedule for a weekly Saturday morning radio show. "I thought it would be fun," he says, echoing what could be described as his life's mantra. Airing live on WHLI, Tom's broadcast is the third-highest-rated radio show on the station. He interviews guests in the studio, covering food topics in an eclectic lineup that reflects Tom's curious, Willy Wonka–ish worldview of food.

Tom creates recipes inspired by his food trips, cooking contemporaries, and garden fresh ingredients. Sometimes he'll envision the entire dish while eating in another chef's restaurant and deconstruct it, using local Long Island fruits, vegetables, and herbs to make it his own; other times it's the raw material that sparks the dish that earns a place on the menu. "I'll stand at the farm in Riverhead and look at the kale or be transported by the fisherman's weakfish in May." He is always inspired by Paumanok Vineyards, whom he partners with for his own Tom Schaudel Reserve– and CoolFish-labeled wines.

At Paumanok Vineyards, a second-generation Long Island family–owned vineyard producing estate-grown wines, Kareem Massoud grew up right along with the grapevines, learning all about local viticulture from his father and by traveling and studying at some of the world's greatest wine-growing locales. He manages the seventy-two-acre vineyard's operations, maximizing its dedication to sustainable growing practices, including the use of solar power. "Here, you can truly experience the fruits of your labor," he says, describing the sense of gratification and community involvement those efforts provide.

In the future, Tom Schaudel sees no retirement. "Why, when I'm having this much fun?" he teases. He wants to develop some more food businesses with his daughter, Courtney, to mentor her and others. Tom says he'll probably settle in the North Fork because of its slower pace and proximity to the sea, vineyards, and farms.

Fried Oyster Bay Oysters with
Avocado Relish and Passion Fruit Fire Oil

Serves 4

2 ripe avocados
2 plum tomatoes, blanched, peeled, seeded, and diced
1/4 c. red onion, finely diced
1 Serrano chile, seeded and minced
1 garlic clove, minced
2 tbsp. cilantro, finely chopped
juice of two limes
1/4 c. passion fruit juice
1/4 tsp. cayenne pepper
1/4 c. soy oil
1 c. olive oil
1 c. Wondra flour
salt and pepper, to taste
1 doz. Blue Point oysters

For the relish: Peel and pit the avocados, place them in a non-reactive bowl, and mash with a fork. Fold in the tomato, red onion, chile, garlic, cilantro, and lime juice. Add an avocado pit to the mixture, cover with plastic wrap, and set aside.

For the fire oil: Place the passion fruit juice and the cayenne pepper in a blender. With the blade running add the soy oil in a slow stream until the mixture is emulsified; set aside.

For the oysters: Heat the olive oil in a large heavy-bottomed pan to 375 degrees. Whisk the flour and salt and pepper together in a shallow dish. Toss the oysters to coat them with the flour mixture, shaking off any excess, and drop them carefully into the oil. Fry until golden (2 to 3 minutes), remove with a slotted spoon, and drain on paper towels to absorb excess oil. Place the avocado relish in the center of the plate. Arrange 3 oysters around the relish, and drizzle with the passion fruit fire oil.

Up-Island Lobster Risotto

with Summer Corn, Heirloom Tomato, and Basil

Serves 8

4 c. lobster stock

4 tbsp. butter

1 c. onion, diced

1 c. Vialone Nano or Aborio rice

4 lobsters, about 1 1/4 lb. each, steamed, meat removed from the shell

1 c. mixed heirloom cherry tomatoes

1/2 c. fresh sweet corn

2 tbsp. fresh basil

In a nonreactive pot, bring the lobster stock to a simmer and maintain it throughout the preparation. In a large sauté pan, melt the butter and sauté the onion until it is translucent. Add the rice, and stir to coat it completely with the butter. Cook the rice, stirring frequently, for 2 minutes without any liquid to toast the kernels. Add 1/2 c. stock, stirring constantly, and cook until the stock is absorbed. Repeat this process until all the stock has been absorbed and the rice is tender to the bite. Stir in the lobster meat, tomatoes, sweet corn, and basil and heat through. Serve in pasta bowls, and garnish with fresh basil leaves.

Strawberry-Rhubarb Shortcake

with Tahitian Vanilla Cream

Serves 6

1 1/3 c. flour

3 tbsp. sugar

1 1/2 tsp. baking powder

1/2 tsp. salt

5 tbsp. butter, chilled and cut into 1/4-inch pieces

2/3 c. cream, plus additional for brushing

2 pt. whole strawberries, hulled

1 lb. rhubarb, cut into 1/2-inch dice

1/2 c. sugar

2 c. Tahitian vanilla whipped cream

4 beans scraped from vanilla bean pod (1 bean per 1 c. cream)

2 tbsp. sugar (1 tbsp. sugar per 1 c. cream)

Preheat the oven to 350 degrees. In a small bowl, whisk together the flour, 2 tbsp. sugar, baking powder, and salt. Add the chilled butter, and cut it into the dry ingredients with a pastry knife until the mixture is crumbly. Add cream and stir with a spoon until the dough comes together. Roll the dough 1 inch thick, and cut out rounds with a cookie cutter. Brush with additional cream, and bake for 7 to 10 minutes. Remove and cool. Mix 1 pt. strawberries, rhubarb, and sugar, together in a saucepan, and cook until the rhubarb has softened and the mixture is a sauce-like consistency. Remove from the fire, and cool. Slice the remaining strawberries, and reserve them in a bowl. Slice the cakes in half horizontally, and top each bottom half with 1/2 c. whipped cream. Divide the strawberries between the cakes and replace the tops. Whip the vanilla beans into the cream and sugar until peaks form. Spoon the strawberry-rhubarb sauce around the plate, garnish, and serve.

Swallow

Chef James Tchinnis

Bee Sting Honey

One may be forgiven for not readily seeing the link between a swallow (as in the bird), a sailor, and eating. It is a delightful discovery, however, not unlike the way guests feel when they eat at Swallow restaurant in Huntington, Long Island.

Why a swallow? Chef James Tchinnis, owner and executive chef, says he chose the swallow icon and name for two reasons: the popular sailor's tattoo of a swallow stands for land or home, and one has to swallow to eat!

The double meaning represents the creative and lighthearted commitment that James and his partner and wife, Julie, bring to establishing a restaurant that is like home: meaning casual and fun, but also a place to eat the very best, fresh-from-the-garden, local food.

Purposefully, James chose a restaurant design that provided an open kitchen. "I wanted my guests to be able to see me cooking and plating the food—just like in a home kitchen. I enjoy chatting with my guests too," he says. The restaurant earned its stars from Long Island *Newsday* shortly after it opened in the fall of 2010 along with rave reviews from Joan Starkey, the *New York Times* expert Long Island restaurant critic.

When James was considering careers at college in the early '90s, he was studying philosophy and art. During a talk with his mother about what he'd do with his life, she suggested he consider becoming a chef. A chef? It wasn't thought of as glamorous at the time, but the more they talked, the more it seemed to make sense to him. His grandfather had been a cook, and the family owned the Turndale Diner in Farmingdale, Long Island. Soon enough James graduated from the French Culinary Institute in Manhattan, having studied under Chef Jacques Pepin. "He reminded me of my grandfather because he used all fresh, natural ingredients. I really identified with that approach," James recalls. "In fact, I thought my knowledge about all the fresh quality ingredients made me a big shot," he jokes self-effacingly. The school was all culinary, all day, nine hours a day, five days a week, for eight months.

And he loved it.

In terms of rationalizing French classic cooking (some would say it's contrived) with the sustainable, simple, pure cooking cuisine he practices today, James explains he believes it is paramount to learn the classic, basic foundation to culinary art and then, with that strong foundation, develop a food repertoire that is different and unique to the chef.

Swallow restaurant has its own garden. Just like home. "To me, a garden *means* home, family, and food!" Here in his own garden he can grow more herbs, lettuces, and tomatoes. "Being Italian, I respect the tomato so much," says James. He uses fresh tomatoes straight from the vine with his fresh oregano and basil.

His commitment to local extends to local farmers and artisanal food producers including Sally Nadler and her homemade honey. Sally's interest in beekeeping was sparked by love. Her father had taken up beekeeping in his retirement and she thought tending her own hives would be a way to honor him and carry on a mutual interest. Beekeeping was also a path to good health for her and her children. Sally had been successfully practicing bee sting therapy to ameliorate the pain from a wrist injury brought about by playing tennis. It worked. The more she learned about the healing properties of bees and their honey, the more she found it was a perfectly natural remedy for her children's allergies—eliminating the need for chemical-based inhalants. Further, the bees' healing properties provide effective natural antibodies—a front-line defense that helps her friends and family ward off disease and illness, much like eating locally grown foods does. It's Nature's way of reminding humans that homegrown is best—for health and well being.

And oh, there is the taste.

The honey made by Sally's beautiful bees is a kind of carbon dating that reflects the food source of a season or time. "Some years I'm told the honey is spicy—a warm feeling in the throat. Other years the liquid gold is sweet, almost citrusy." Ultimately, the plants, the climate, and the water influence the taste. "These are not one-note honey bees. The nectar is a Long Island brew that tastes like the blend of local flower nectars from a five-mile radius." Sweet! And exciting inspiration for James.

Sally enthusiastically notes that James was her first chef client.

"I was giving my honey to friends, and a mutual friend gave some to James," Sally recalls. In fact, James was her first paying customer for Bee Sting Honey, she nods with gleeful pride. "Chef James—or Jimmy—bought two to three gallons in the beginning of that season." Pretty much all she had to offer.

James believes Long Island will continue to grow as a food destination for a number of reasons. "Being just outside of Manhattan—that is the center of the food universe—we have a big brother/little brother relationship. As chefs, we want the respect. We want to make a name for ourselves too. Plus we have all of nature: the best beaches, theater, and a lot of culture," he adds with homegrown pride.

Roasted Beets, House-Made Ricotta, Baby Carrots, and Honey

Serves 4

2 medium-sized beets
8 baby carrots
4 tbsp. kosher salt (divided)
1 qt. whole milk
2 c. buttermilk
2 tbsp. heavy cream
1 tbsp. fresh thyme leaves (picked from stem)
4 tbsp. local honey
4 tbsp. extra virgin olive oil
1 tsp. cracked black pepper
3 pieces of cheesecloth

Preheat the oven to 375 degrees. Roast the beets in the oven on a baking tray for 1 hour or until fork tender. Let cool slightly, and peel under running water. Chill until ready to use.

Place the carrots in a pot, and cover with cold water and 3 tbsp. kosher salt. Bring to a boil, then lower to a simmer. Cook until carrots are fork tender (about 3 minutes after the water boils). Chill under cold water until ready to use.

Place milk, buttermilk, heavy cream, and 1/2 tbsp. salt in pot, and heat on medium to low heat until it just starts to bubble, stirring with wooden spoon every 3 minutes. Turn off, and let the mixture sit for 4 minutes. Skim off all the solids, and place the liquid in a cheesecloth in a colander to drain excess liquid; after 2 minutes of draining, gather the corners of the cloth and press the cheese into a ball and refrigerate.

To prepare: Slice beets into 1/4-inch rounds, and arrange 2 slices on a plate with a spoonful of cheese and 2 baby carrots. Drizzle each with local honey and olive oil, and season with thyme, remaining salt, and pepper.

Swallow's "Mac & Cheese"
with Asiago Béchamel

Serves 4

- 1/2 lb. thick-cut bacon, cut crosswise into small pieces
- 1/2 lb. orzo
- 3/4 c. fresh peas, blanched and chilled
- 3 c. Asiago Béchamel Sauce
- good Parmesan for grating

Sauté the bacon in a pan until crisp, drain fat, and reserve bacon to the side. Cook the orzo in salted water until al dente. Add the bacon and peas to the Asiago Béchamel Sauce, pour it over the orzo, and mix. Grate Parmesan over the top. Be generous with the cheese.

ASIAGO BÉCHAMEL SAUCE:
- 2 tbsp. sweet butter (divided)
- 1 tbsp. flour
- 1 c. whole milk
- 2 c. heavy cream
- 2 tsp. kosher salt
- 1/2 tsp. white pepper
- 1 c. Asiago cheese, grated

Melt 1 tbsp. butter in a saucepan, and whisk in flour until combined. Cook for 1 minute, and add milk, heavy cream, salt, and pepper while whisking. Continue whisking and cooking until thickened (about 5 minutes more). When the sauce is thick, take it off the heat and whisk in the cheese and the remaining butter until it is smooth.

Black Angus Sliders
with Tomato Jam

Serves 4

- 1/2 tbsp. fresh ginger, chopped
- 1/2 tbsp. garlic, chopped
- 1 tbsp. vegetable oil
- 1/2 c. cider vinegar
- 2 cans (28 oz. each) whole peeled tomatoes
- 1 cinnamon stick
- 1 c. granulated sugar
- 1/2 c. local honey
- 1 1/2 lb. Angus ground beef (formed into 8 sliders, 3 oz. each)
- pinch salt
- pepper
- 8 Martin's dinner rolls

Sauté the ginger and garlic in a deep-sided saucepan in oil for 1 minute. Add vinegar and reduce by three-quarters. Add tomatoes, cinnamon stick, and sugar, and cook on medium heat for about 1/2 an hour or until almost all the tomato juice is gone. Remove from the heat, discard the cinnamon stick, and add the honey. Chill until cold.

Season the burgers with salt and pepper, and cook on a grill or in a skillet to desired doneness (2 minutes per side for medium rare). Place the meat on buns and top with a generous helping of cold, delicious tomato jam.

Kitchen A Bistro and Kitchen A Trattoria

Chef Eric Lomando
Kitchen A Bistro Garden

If the devil is in the details, Chef Eric Lomando's recipes are sinfully spot-on.

He consistently refers to "an obsession with improving"; taking little steps along the way to make the food and garden better. Curiously, despite the restless pursuit of his ever-elusive standard of excellence just over the rainbow, he is quite spiritual about his quest for food nirvana.

"Not to get overly virtuous about the environment and its connection to cooking and food, but I do feel a responsibility to the oceans and to the land."

It is that passion for sustainable and renewable natural resources that makes his intense style of cooking with the best local, seasonal ingredients possible. His reverence for nearby food and his gastronomic artistry turn the best of Long Island's farms and oceans into his distinctive cuisine. Eric has earned a #1 rating from Zagat as the best of Long Island, and a coveted three stars from *Newsday*'s knowledgeable restaurant critic.

Eric's dedication to continuous improvement has brought him a long way from his start as a busboy at age fourteen, voraciously eating the food at the restaurant. It was so much more interesting than the suburban American fare at home. It wasn't long before he moved on to be a line cook. The adrenaline and the energy in the kitchen drew him to the restaurant and cooking lifestyle, along with the realization that it was so "addictively motivating. It's definitely exhausting: all consuming," says Eric.

He acknowledges one of the most important jobs for him is continually to train his line cooks to achieve his culinary vision, to mentor them, and to inspire them to seek ongoing, self-motivated improvement. And his nearly twenty staff members are infused with his harnessed fire and passion. "I am driving them to do better—to look at serving or cooking with pride. No standing around."

Hardly.

Eric was dining at Kitchen A Bistro in 1999 when a conversation with the restaurant's then chef-owner led to a job there. Not surprisingly, his personal food quest drove him to cook food *his* way.

In June 2000, with the ink barely dry on his diploma, Eric bought the eight-hundred-square-foot, thirty-seat Bistro just six months after graduating from culinary school at the New York Institute of Technology in Islip.

But that was just the first chip on the table. In a bit of what could be called the Long Island restaurant shuffle, Eric relocated Kitchen A Bistro down the road to a larger location, the former spot of Long Island's landmark restaurant, Mirabelle. He then established Kitchen A Trattoria in the original space, opening in spring 2009.

Eric always knew he'd grow a garden at his restaurant, and when he bought the second space for Kitchen A Bistro, he inherited the garden that had been Chef Guy Reuge's Mirabelle potager. Today, the

Bistro garden boasts turnips, "tons of potatoes," radishes, tomatoes, herbs, Swiss chard, beans, and lettuces. Eric's father-in-law, Bill Pisano, a lifelong gardener of Italian descent, has turned the plot into a world-class kitchen garden beginning with a dedicated attention to the soil. He grows herbs and heirloom tomato varieties as well as heirloom eggplants and cucumbers. Eric and Bill share a mutual respect for each other and for the quality of food. "I understand what he wants and in turn, I let him know what produce is good," explains Bill. And the customers at Kitchen A Bistro know and appreciate the just-picked, garden fresh vegetables Bill nurtures from plant to plate.

Eric is a back-to-basics chef. He steers clear of food fads, yet stays on point keeping up with current food trends and news. The quality of local, sustainable food gives him an advantage before he even touches it. "It's no secret that a pasture-raised chicken compared to a Perdue is just so much better," Eric says. He's learned to use his chef's pulpit to help farmers garner the monetary compensation they deserve for their work and to help create demand for their harvest. "I'm out in the dining rooms talking to our customers about the responsibility we have for access to our food," Eric states. "And the service staff consistently reinforces the reason the food tastes better is because of the origin or provenance of the ingredients," he adds.

Eric describes his flavor style as Mediterranean. He explains that while Long Island had a lot of Italian restaurants, he thought there was a dearth of real Italian cuisine with its focus on simple, pure recipes that revere fresh, quality, seasonal ingredients. He wanted to pursue and perfect that eating sensibility. "As a chef, I believe it's key to express yourself and cook food *you* like to eat," he explains. "I like to eat Italian."

Eric's style of local food is an intensified focus on seasonality. He changes the menu every day at both restaurants. His most challenging season is winter, but he overcomes what can be perceived as a dead season with creativity, using hearty root vegetables, such as butternut squash with mozzarella on a tasting menu, along with kale, hearty stews, braised meats and bay scallops. Developing recipes for this season appeals to his sense of pushing the envelope and trying to improve. In addition, delighting his customers is the ultimate reward.

Halibut with Summer Tomatoes

Serves 4

10 vine-ripened tomatoes
salt
3 tbsp. olive oil
3–4 tbsp. Banyuls vinegar
4 pieces halibut, about 5 oz. each
salt, pepper, olive oil, and basil, to season

Slice 1 tomato into thin rounds; you should get at least eight slices. Place the sliced tomatoes on a sheet tray, season with salt and olive oil, and place in an oven set to the lowest possible temperature. Allow the rounds to dry for at least 5 hours. Chop 5 of the remaining tomatoes coarsely; season with salt and 3 to 4 tbsp. vinegar. Allow the chopped tomatoes to marinate for about 1 hour.

Pass chopped tomatoes through a juicer. Place the juice in a sauce-pot, and bring it to a boil over low heat. Skim off the foam that rises to the top, and discard. You should be left with about 1 pt. of tomato consommé.

Place the dried tomato pieces over halibut, and arrange in a steamer basket. Set the steamer over boiling water, and cover. The fish should steam in approximately 5 to 7 minutes. Check doneness by inserting a metal skewer into the center of the fish and touching it to your lip. The skewer should feel warm to the touch.

While the fish is steaming, slice the remaining tomatoes and season them with salt and pepper, olive oil, a touch more Banyuls vinegar, and basil. Place the fish on top of the tomatoes, and sauce with tomato consommé. The sauce can be served hot or cold, depending on your preference.

Polentina with Spring Vegetables
(Polenta Soup)

Serves 4

- 2 qt. well-flavored chicken stock (can use vegetable stock for a vegetarian soup)
- salt and pepper, to taste
- 1 c. slow-roasted polenta (from Anson Mills)
- assorted spring vegetables, blanched in salted water and refreshed in ice water (asparagus, fava beans, English peas, ramps, and morels)
- Parmigiano Reggiano, to garnish
- olive oil, to garnish

Bring the chicken stock to a boil, reduce to medium heat, and season to taste with salt and pepper. Add the polenta in a steady stream, whisking constantly to avoid any lumps. Simmer the broth for at least 1 hour. Add the spring vegetables to the soup and allow it to simmer for 2 minutes to heat through. Serve and garnish with Parmigiano and extra virgin olive oil.

Butternut Squash Saltimbocca
with Burrata Cheese

Serves 4

- 8 sage leaves
- 4 pieces of butternut squash, cut into planks about 2x1x1/2 inches
- 8 pieces imported prosciutto
- canola oil
- 1 ball burrata cheese
- aged balsamic vinegar
- extra virgin olive oil

Place two sage leaves (stem removed) on top of each piece of butternut squash, and then wrap completely around with prosciutto. Cover the bottom of a pan with canola oil, and sauté each wrapped squash Saltimbocca. When the prosciutto has been crisped on all sides, place the pieces in a 375-degree oven for 5 to 7 minutes.

Place the squash in the center of 4 warmed plates. Cut the burrata into quarters, and place it on top of the squash. (Use the creamy liquid that comes out when you cut it on the plate as well. It is delicious.) Garnish with a drizzle of aged balsamic and extra virgin olive oil. Serve while hot.

Restaurant Mirabelle & Tavern Mirabelle

Chef Guy Reuge
Mirabelle Garden

Guy Reuge is the classic French cook, brilliant in his *métier*, steadfast in his adherence to technique, and mentor to the next cohort of home-grown chefs. By introducing Long Island residents to fresh, good food, Guy has defined Long Island's culinary landscape for generations.

Long ago, Guy earned the respect of his customers and purveyors, picking up his share of accolades along the way. In 2001, the French minister of agriculture awarded Guy the medal of Le Mérite Agricole for his support and dedication to traditional farming in this country. In 2006, Guy was awarded the coveted Le Toque d'Argent that crowns a master chef of France in America for lifelong achievement.

Guy grew up in the Loire Valley not long after World War II near the biggest U.S. Army base in Europe. He remembers being utterly fascinated by an American family who moved from the base to their own house not far from his family's home. The Americans had a barbecue in the yard where they roasted marshmallows and ate flat, sliced Wonder Bread! The whole tableau left an indelible impression, and he vowed to go to America someday.

Back in his own yard, he was busy tending the garden. In French tradition, when a child reached twelve years of age, he or she was given a part of the family garden to maintain. He remembers bringing carrots with the dirt still on them and strawberries still warm from the sun into the kitchen.

In the meantime, his family determined he was to become a cook. The three-year, hands-on cooking apprenticeships in France always began at around age fourteen. Eventually, Guy earned a Certificate of Professional Aptitude and immediately joined the Compagnons du Tour de France to work in top-tier restaurants in northern France and in Paris, achieving much success. But still looming in his mind's eye was that exotic American family.

Soon, Guy was able to secure a position in New York City cooking with George Rey at a Swiss restaurant. After about two years, he began what was to be the first chapter of several tenured stays in New York, followed by a return to France and then a boomerang back to America.

It was *amour* that brought him back to New York for good when he met Maria, his future wife, then an editor at *Gourmet* magazine. Maria introduced him to her associate, *Gourmet*'s food editor, Sally Darr. Together, Sally and Guy collaborated on *Gourmet's France*, the magazine's first French cookbook.

After the book was published, Sally contacted Guy to help her and her husband, John, open their La Tulipe restaurant in New York's Greenwich Village. The eatery earned rave reviews and great success, but despite the acclaim, Guy was restless to move on.

After a few years, his wife's Long Island family approached the couple to join them in a restaurant venture there. "I wanted to have a French country restaurant. I wanted to work in my own garden," he says now. "Early on, I was already thinking of the relationships with the farmers."

For six months he and Maria looked for a place before hitting upon an old farmhouse poised on five acres. "I said, 'This is it!' It had a place for a garden too."

As soon as they closed the deal, they put in tomatoes, various garden green beans, and herbs. "It was like being home in the Loire Valley to put in a garden and go from cooking to garden and garden to cooking," Guy recalls with satisfied glee. They opened Mirabelle in 1983 with Guy in the kitchen and Maria managing the front of the house. The restaurant was an unmitigated and widely acclaimed success.

In 2009, Guy closed Mirabelle in St. James, and the gastronomic gasps were heard from Syosset to Southold. He now works for Lessings, Inc., a storied food company founded in 1890, for which he hopes to open other restaurants and develop corporate dining room menus. He is most thrilled, however, to have redefined and reopened the beloved Long Island landmark Mirabelle—and doing it one better, according to Guy. "Why do one Mirabelle restaurant when two is *meilleure*?" There are now *deux* Mirabelles: Restaurant Mirabelle and Mirabelle Tavern. The restaurant duo is part of the Three Village Inn, which is a mainstay of any Long Island food destination.

David Marzano, Mirabelle's beer and spirits manager, lovingly tends Mirabelle's garden. Following a childhood spent working in the family garden and an inspired trip to England and France, it wasn't long after David Marzano started working for Guy that he eagerly embraced gardening in the raised beds to accommodate an ever-expanding interest in fresh foods for the Mirabelle kitchen. All together, Mirabelle grows more than fifty varieties of fresh produce, and David uses the fresh herbs and garden flavors in the masterful, sophisticated cocktails he creates with North Shore alchemy.

And while Guy changes the menu seasonally and is always creating, he retains some core favorite recipes, with a twist. But he still will never cook out of season. "The season dictates the menu," Guy states emphatically. He then describes how much more fun it is to cook and eat with the rhythm of nature.

It seems that in the end, Guy found a way to recreate the drama of that dreamy, fascinating American lifestyle he observed so long ago—built on a foundation that unites French and Long Island terroir and a passion for homegrown food.

Hoisin-Glazed Grass-Fed Beef Filet

Serves 6

1 1/2 lb. Yukon Gold potatoes, peeled
salt and pepper, to season
1 c. milk
4 oz. sweet butter
pinch (or 1/4–1/2 tsp.) nutmeg, shaved
1/2 lb. sugar peas
1/2 lb. snow peas
1 lb. sweet garden peas
6 grass-fed beef filets, 6 oz. each
1/2 c. hoisin
1/3 c. chicken stock
6 shallots, sliced
2 c. beer batter
1 small tube wasabi paste

Potato purée: Cut the potatoes into large pieces, and cook them in water with salt until soft. Pour the milk in a small pot with the butter and shaved nutmeg. When cooked, drain the potatoes and pass them through a food mill. Add some of the milk mixture in order to obtain the smooth consistency of a purée. Rectify the seasoning (meaning salt and pepper to taste), cover, and keep hot.

Peas: Clean the sugar and snow peas, blanch them rapidly in salted boiling water, and cool down in ice cold water. Drain and cut the peas into small pieces. Blanch the sweet peas using the same method as above; drain and reserve juice. Combine the peas, and set aside 1 c. Put the remaining peas in a blender, and process to obtain a smooth purée. Pass the mixture through a China cap, and set aside.

Beef: Season each beef filet with salt and pepper on each side. Cook them in a frying pan to rare. Remove the excess fat from the pan, put back the filets, and add the hoisin and the chicken stock. Reduce the sauce, turning the meat around in the pan until it is nicely glazed and cooked to medium rare.

Combine the cup of reserved peas with the potato purée, and add just enough pea juice to obtain a bright green color. Rectify seasoning. Dip the shallots in beer batter, and deep fry. Combine some pea juice with the wasabi, and set aside.

To serve: Place the purée in the center of the plates, top with the beef filets, drizzle the glaze on and around the steaks. Add some fried shallots on top of each filet, and add a small spoonful of wasabi/pea juice around the plates.

Wild Mushroom Cappuccino

Serves 8

2 oz. sweet butter
1/2 c. shallot, sliced
1 clove garlic, crushed
1/3 c. port wine
1 lb. wild mushrooms (choose according to the season),
  cleaned and roughly chopped
salt and pepper
1 qt. chicken stock
1 c. crème fraîche
milk for the foam
porcini powder
croutons toasted with Parmesan cheese, to serve

Heat up a small pot, add the butter, and let it melt. Add the shallot and garlic, cover, and let simmer over medium-low heat. Stir from time to time, and cook for about 10 minutes.

Bring the pot to a higher heat, and deglaze with the port wine. Add the mushrooms, season with salt and pepper, cover, and cook for 10 more minutes, still stirring. Add the chicken stock and bring to a boil. Cook for 30 minutes. Add the crème fraîche and bring the mixture back to a quick boil.

Transfer the mixture to a blender, and pass it through a fine china cap strainer. Rectify the seasoning, and keep it hot until serving. If you have a cappuccino machine, foam the milk in the traditional way, or use a hand froth machine. Pour the cappuccino into demi-tasse cups, top each cup with the froth and a sprinkle of porcini powder, and serve with Parmesan croutons.

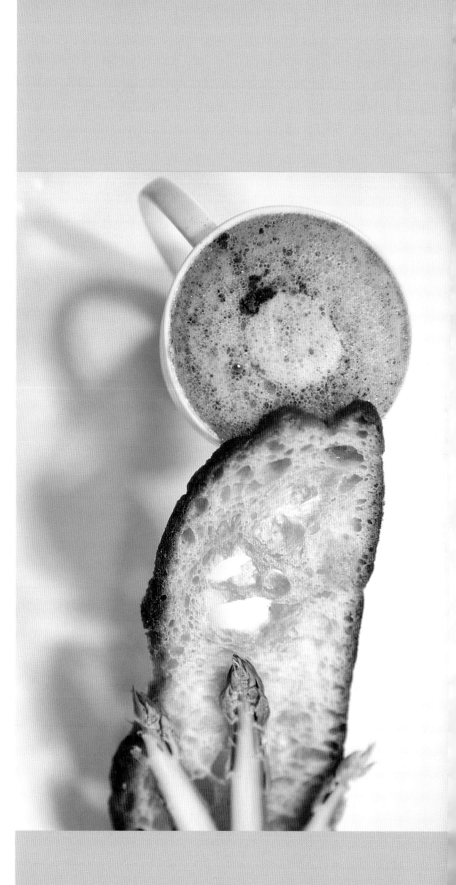

Summer Blueberry Tart

Serves 6

DOUGH:
- **2 c. plus 1 tbsp. flour**
- **1 1/4 c. sugar**
- **1 stick plus 1 tbsp. (or 9 tbsp.) butter**
- **1 large egg**

Sift the flour, sugar, and salt together. In a mixer fitted with a paddle, combine all of the ingredients. Remove the dough from the bowl, form a ball, cover, and refrigerate for a few hours.

Roll the dough to mold sixteen 3-inch-diameter tart molds. Freeze the tartlet shells before baking them in a 350-degree oven for about 10 minutes or until they turn golden.

BLUEBERRY COMPOTE:
- **4 pt. blueberries**
- **2/3 c. of sugar**

In a small pot, combine 2 pt. blueberries and sugar. Place the pot on the stove, and stir until the mixture appears to be cooked and liquefies slightly. Remove from the stove, and add the remaining 2 pt. blueberries to the cooked mixture. Refrigerate rapidly.

At serving time, add a few spoonfuls of Blueberry Compote to the prebaked tartlet shells, top with a scoop of honey or vanilla ice cream, and a small amount of raspberry coulis to decorate each plate.

Fizzy Strawberry-Basil Lemonade
(non-alcoholic)

Serves 4

This unique drink provides a refreshing way to enjoy the delicious fruits from the strawberry patch that come in from May to July combined with slightly spicy and citrusy lemon basil. It is perfect on a hot summer afternoon after doing a few outdoor chores.

20–25 strawberries (depending on their size)

juice of 6 large lemons

water, as needed

ice

25 medium-sized lemon basil leaves

6 tbsp. simple syrup (equal parts granulated sugar and water
  brought to a boil then allowed to cool)

24 oz. club soda, approximately

4 sprigs lemon basil, for garnish

TOOLS NEEDED:

4 hi-ball glasses

1 blender

1 large spoon

1 bar shaker

1 coil strainer

Remove the stems from the strawberries, and add them to the blender with the juice from 2 lemons and a few tablespoons of water, enough to get the strawberries to purée. Set aside.

In the bar shaker, add several ice cubes, the remaining lemon juice, and the basil leaves. Shake well for 30 seconds to release the aromatics from the basil. Strain the lemon basil–infused juice into the strawberry purée. Add the simple syrup and stir to incorporate.

Fill the hi-ball glasses with ice, and add a quarter of the strawberry mixture to each glass. Stir in the club soda, garnish with the basil sprig, and enjoy!

Amarelle Restaurant

Chef Lia Fallon
Andrews Family Farm

Lia's mother admonished her often, "Do not run faster than your guardian angel can fly!" But after waiting what seemed like half her life to develop her not-to-be-denied passion of working with food, she's not looking over her shoulder.

Today, Lia is a chef, caterer, cooking teacher, and food stylist. After launching her career with the Food Network, she began consulting and developing recipes for several food councils and advising on commercials as well.

What drives a wife and mother of two to heed the siren song of culinary art?

The answer no doubt involves the love of food and the excitement of discovery and flavor, along with pride in her family's heritage of farming on Long Island.

When Lia's Italian great grandparents settled in the area, they intended to establish a homestead for future generations, buying more than enough land for their eleven children and their progeny to call this place home. Today, most of what remains of that land is Sanzoverino Lane, and Lia's entire family still lives there in Bayville.

Lia's foundation of family, food, and entertaining underscores all that she does. Despite Lia's more than fifteen years of success at owning and running a day spa that her father urged her to establish, her first love was food.

"I always got very excited for the events at the spa: planning the menu, decorating, preparing the food platters. Not to mention family holidays and special occasions where I could create delicious food that was gorgeous to look at," Lia explains.

Eventually, she enrolled in the Culinary Academy of Long Island in Syosset. The school's curriculum demanded a three-month externship, and without hesitation, she knew where she was headed. It was 2003, and the popularity of live TV cooking shows was electrifying the country and making celebrities out of cooks and chefs.

But how did Lia secure such a coveted position with the Food Network? "I was persistent. I wrote letters asking them to pick me," she now says very matter of factly.

Persistence paid off. She finally was invited to participate in a full day of interviews with the executive chef of the network and a number of other key people. As if that weren't intimidating enough, Lia had to cook lunch for the executive chef and his staff of twelve. Maybe her love of cooking and entertaining was so consuming that the audience didn't hold any undue worries for her, but regardless, she got the job!

Lia worked in all aspects of production and behind the scenes work, including recipe development, food styling, and staging. She was also cooking through recipes in the test kitchen for shows such as Rachel Ray's *30 Minute Meals,* Sandra Lee's *Semi-Homemade Cooking*, and Bobby Flay's *Boy Meets Grill*, as well as setting up for Emeril Lagasse's shows. Lia's successful results and networking

contacts at the Food Network led to a full-time freelance position for two years, working in production.

At the same time, the tight-knit food community began recommending Lia for other opportunities, including food styling for a number of important commercial photo shoots. "One thing led to another," Lia says. "From HGTV, I got the job for a GMC commercial, and Jose Cuervo tequila. From Sandra Lee, I was able to secure first the California Fig Board, which then snowballed to work for other food boards."

Soon, back on Long Island, a new Viking school opened at Anna Pump's Bridgehampton Inn, and Lia signed on to teach recreational cooking to adults and children. It was a wonderful experience for both the students and the teacher, she remembers. She also met fellow teacher Steve Biscari-Amaral at the school.

Lia and Steve formed a working relationship through Black Tie Caterers and, for more than two years, successfully catered weddings in the vineyards of the North Fork. Later they worked at consulting, revamping East End restaurant menus—bringing local, fresh food recipes to the menu offerings. Business was so good that by the summer of 2009 both recognized that they needed—and wanted—a restaurant of their own. Amarelle Restaurant opened to rave reviews the following year, with the *New York Times*' Joanne Starkey rating it "excellent" and writing glowingly of her "memorable meal." With culinary ascendancy, Lia took over the quaint country restaurant in 2010.

Securing local purveyors for the restaurant was something Lia embraced from the beginning, and she is particularly inspired by the Andrews Family Farm, a beautiful heritage farm located not far from the restaurant where she gives on-site cooking demonstrations. Denise Andrews, part owner of Andrews Farm, has a degree in art, a talent on full display in the ornamental flower baskets and the rich, textural food compositions at Andrews' Farmstand. The members of the Andrews family deliver the daily harvest themselves to Manhattan, retaining about a quarter of it for sale at their farmstand and other local stands. The Andrews children work the farm too, and one son is studying agriculture at Cornell University. With each new generation, they continue Long Island's family farm heritage.

Lia's enthusiasm for all things food is contagious. Soon after meeting her, newfound friends are eager to stop at nothing to get the best ingredients, taste more, learn more, meet more foodies. There just isn't enough time to take it all in. In fact, even her guardian angel might be forgiven for taking time to rest and enjoy one of Lia's delicious homegrown meals.

Peach and Seasonal Berry Cobbler

Serves 6–8

1 c. all-purpose flour
1/2 c. white sugar
2 tsp. baking powder
1/2 c. cold butter, cut in pea-size cubes
1/2 c. milk
1 c. granola
1/4 c. packed brown sugar
1 tbsp. cornstarch
1/2 c. cold water
3 c. fresh peaches, peeled, pitted, and sliced
2 c. fresh assorted berries
1 tbsp. butter
1 tbsp. lemon juice
2 tbsp. coarse granulated sugar
1/4 tsp. ground nutmeg

Preheat the oven to 375 degrees. In a medium bowl, stir together the flour, white sugar, and baking powder. Mix in the butter until the mixture becomes crumbly. Add in the milk, and fold in the granola.

In a medium saucepan, stir together the brown sugar, cornstarch, and water. Mix in the peaches and assorted berries. Cook and stir over medium heat until thick and bubbly. Mix in 1 tbsp. butter and lemon juice. Continue cooking until the butter melts. Pour into a 1 1/2-qt. ungreased baking dish. Evenly spoon the batter in mounds over the hot fruit. In a small bowl, mix the coarse sugar and nutmeg, and sprinkle it over the batter.

Place the baking dish on a shallow baking pan in the preheated oven. Bake the cobbler for about 25 minutes, or until bubbly and a toothpick inserted into the crust comes out clean. Serve warm with vanilla gelato or whipped cream.

Stuffed Squash Blossoms

Serves 4

12 fresh zucchini or other edible squash blossoms
8 oz. (1 c.) Catapano Farms goat cheese, softened
1 tbsp. extra virgin olive oil, plus extra for tossing
zest of 1 lemon
1/4 c. fresh herbs: thyme, basil, parsley, chervil, tarragon, dill, cilantro
3 eggs lightly beaten
1 c. flour, seasoned with salt, pepper, and paprika
vegetable oil, for frying
1 pt. baby heirloom tomatoes
smoked sea salt
freshly ground black pepper
aged balsamic vinegar

Inspect the squash blossoms; don't get them wet, but check inside for bugs and soil. Open them gently, as they are fragile. Brush each with a soft clean towel, and remove any insects. Set aside.

Mix the goat cheese with 1 tbsp. olive oil, lemon zest, and the freshly chopped herbs of your choice. Using a pastry bag, place about 1 tbsp. of the goat cheese (less if the blossoms are small) inside each squash blossom. Close the blossom. Dip it in the beaten egg, and the dredge it in the flour mixture.

Heat a large skillet with a medium to high flame, and add 1/2 inch of vegetable oil. When the oil gets hot, pan sear the stuffed blossoms until golden, turning to cook on all sides.

Dice the tomatoes, and lightly toss them with extra virgin olive oil and smoked sea salt and fresh pepper. Serve the tomatoes alongside the blossoms as a garnish. Drizzle with good quality balsamic vinegar.

Ratatouille

Serves 6–8

1/4 c. extra virgin olive oil

2 onions, 1/2-inch dice

4 cloves garlic, minced or crushed

3 bell peppers, cut into 1-inch squares (try different colors)

1 c. white wine

2 eggplants, cut into 1/2-inch cubes

2 zucchini, cut into 1/2-inch cubes

2 yellow squash, cut into 1/2-inch cubes

2 pounds tomatoes, chopped

1 tbsp. fresh thyme, minced

kosher salt and fresh ground pepper, to taste

1/4 c. fresh basil, chopped

1/4 c. Parmesan Reggiano cheese, shaved

Heat the olive oil in a heavy soup pot on medium heat. Add the onions, sauté until golden, and then add the garlic. Cook for about 1 minute to infuse the flavor. Add the bell peppers, and cook until for another 5 minutes. Deglaze the pan with the white wine. Then add the eggplants, zucchini, squash, and tomatoes. Add the thyme leaves, and season with salt and pepper. Stir well and cook 5 minutes. Turn down the heat, and cover the pot. Simmer until everything is soft and well blended—about 30 minutes. Remove from heat, and plate. Garnish with chopped basil and cheese.

The South Shore

Among the oldest regions in the country, Long Island's South Shore extends east from Brooklyn and Queens along the Atlantic Ocean. Here, charming bayside villages and summer resorts cozy up to majestic sandy beaches with quaint nautical ports. Diverse in culture and income, the South Shore has grown from its rural roots to become a great place for food, live music, and fun.

The Lake House

Chef Matt Connors

The Farm at St. Peter's

Chef Matt Connors grew up in Bayshore, just on the other side of Lake Lawrence from where his highly successful restaurant, the Lake House, is nestled today. In the intervening years, his culinary adventures led him to San Francisco, Italy, and New York City. Just how did this understated culinary artist manage to come full circle to settle in his own backyard?

The tale starts when Matt was around fifteen years old. He already knew he wanted to be a chef, so he apprenticed at a few local restaurants, most notably La Mascotte. After graduating from high school, Matt attended the Culinary Institute of America (CIA). For his culinary school externship, he was committed to finding a restaurant distinguished by its fresh, farm-centric environment, and in 1993, San Francisco was on the cutting edge of the emerging farm-to-table food phenomenon.

Matt says, "The city's restaurants, at that time, were way ahead of the curve; even before New York caught on to the farmers' markets, San Francisco was seeing them emerge as established, successful food resources."

Matt secured a line cook position with San Francisco Chef Wolfgang Puck's Postrio restaurant. He learned to source and buy organic, heirloom produce and livestock.

"We got fresh lettuces from a co-op; the restaurant noted the farmers who supplied the ingredients and gave them on-page menu credit," he says.

Upon returning to New York City and receiving his CIA diploma in 1995, he landed a job at Arcadia, Anna Rosenweig's forty-seat restaurant that was getting lots of press. He worked his way up through several other restaurants before helping Scott Bryan establish Veritas restaurant, which debuted in 1999.

That same year, Matt and his wife, Eileen (also a culinary professional), honeymooned in Italy, where they both fell hard for the beauty and lifestyle of the Tuscan region. With the help of the Veritas owners, Matt secured a position for a year with Locanda del Principato, a private dining club outside of Chianti. The Tim Burton–esque country club was open just three days a week, and all diners were served the same eleven-course meal at the same time, dining-hall style. The club's remarkable chef, Richardo Chechini, was a hunter and forager, and Matt eagerly joined him on the daily search for wild asparagus and black truffles, hunting for boar and uccelletti birds (eating the tiny birds has since been banned there).

After he and Eileen returned to New York City in July 2001, Matt again cooked at Veritas, but five years later, when the restaurant was undergoing renovations, the couple had some downtime and decided to open their own restaurant. They thought they had hit pay dirt in the painfully hip neighborhood of Williamsburg, Brooklyn, but in yet in another twist of fortune, the day the contract was to have been finalized, the deal fell apart.

As they were driving home to Long Island to lick their wounds with family, Eileen spotted a new potential restaurant spot that was so down in the dumps Matt had never even visited it. That same day, they found themselves in a handshake deal to take over the place on Lawrence Lake. Only six months later, after the couple had completely gutted the building, the fifty-five-seat Lake House opened for dinner, sporting a coolly elegant décor more akin to an Upper East Side dining establishment than one in suburban Long Island.

For all the right reasons, the Lake House earned great ratings from Zagat and outstanding restaurant reviews from the *New York Times* and *New York Newsday*, all of which helped bolster Matt's reputation as a superior chef proud to feature local, farm-fresh food.

Matt has an excellent relationship with the Farm at St. Peter's, located next to his family's house and around the corner from the restaurant. The farm features only organic crops grown from seed and is committed to sustainable practices and community education. Matt says Eileen and their two children often pick vegetables there and then walk to the restaurant to deliver them. Matt himself goes every day for some items, still hot from the sun when he picks them up.

"While the crop selections are static, we rotate the beds," explains Regina, who, along with her husband, Larry, were the managers of the community-supported agriculture (CSA) program at the farm. "And we introduce select produce every year, such as new eggplant varieties or kale."

When Matt prepares his menus for each season, he might use a version of a dish he created previously, but he constantly infuses it with fresh and new seasonal ingredients. While he says he gets very excited about the ingredients, he also follows a philosophy of "the simpler, the better."

"We try to do as little as possible to the product. From a poached farm-fresh egg to grilled asparagus, locally made goat cheese, and baby arugula, it is the natural purity of the ingredients that makes the food delicious," he says.

The Connors' restaurant is just across the lake from where Matt's personal culinary adventure story began. There, his family had an industrious, twenty-five-square-foot garden. "Eileen and I have the same now, just a bit smaller," Matt says proudly. And his parents are still using their own garden to grow leeks, beets, tomatoes, and herbs for their son's restaurant—right across the lake.

Marinated Natural Lamb Loin with Garden Ratatouille, Goat Cheese Gnocchi, and Herb Vinaigrette

Serves 6

LAMB:

 1 lamb saddle, trimmed of all silverskin by butcher
 2 tbsp. extra virgin olive oil
 1 tbsp. rosemary, chopped
 2 cloves garlic, chopped
 splash red wine

Combine the olive oil, rosemary, garlic, and red wine. Marinate the lamb overnight.

GARDEN RATATOUILLE:

 1 c. eggplant, diced
 1 c. zucchini or yellow squash, diced
 2 cloves garlic, chopped
 1/4 c. very good extra virgin olive oil
 1 roasted red bell pepper, peeled and diced
 1 yellow onion, diced
 1 c. red tomato, skinned, seeded, and chopped
 2 tbsp. sliced basil
 2 tbsp. good balsamic vinegar

Lightly salt and drain the eggplant overnight. (*Chef's note:* This step is optional, but we do it at the Lake House.) Sauté eggplant, zucchini or squash, and garlic in olive oil for 5 minutes or until slightly golden. Add the rest of the ingredients, and simmer slowly for 20 minutes. Remove from the heat, and add balsamic vinegar.

GOAT CHEESE GNOCCHI:

 8 oz. fresh goat cheese (*Chef's note:* We use Catapano Dairy
   Farm cheese from the North Fork of Long Island.)
 1 egg
 pinch of salt
 1/2 c. flour (up to 1 c.)
 1 tbsp. extra virgin olive oil

In a large mixing bowl, combine the goat cheese, egg, and a generous pinch of salt. Beat with a stiff whisk until the mixture is smooth. Begin by adding 1/2 c. flour, gently kneading it in. Continue adding flour 1 tbsp. at a time, up to a full cup, until the first sign of a malleable nonsticky mass of dough appears. Do not add too much flour or overknead; the dough should be soft, airy, and very light. Cover the dough, and refrigerate for 30 minutes.

Bring a large pot of lightly salted water to a boil. Set aside a large bowl of ice water. On a lightly floured surface, roll out the dough into a rectangle 1/2 inch thick. Using a long knife, cut the dough into 1/2-inch-by-1-inch pieces. Place the pieces on a floured tray; continue until all dough is cut. Boil the gnocchi immediately until they are fluffy and firm, 2 to 3 minutes. Using a slotted spoon, transfer them to the ice water bath. As soon as gnocchi are cool, drain and set aside. Brown gently in olive oil and serve.

HERB VINAIGRETTE:

 1 c. packed green basil
 1 c. packed flat leaf parsley
 2 shallots, minced fine
 zest and juice of 1 lemon
 2 tbsp. white wine vinegar
 6 tbsp. extra virgin olive oil
 salt and pepper, to taste

Chop basil and parsley as fine as possible. Mix in the rest of the ingredients. Season with salt and pepper.

To serve: Spoon some Garden Ratatouille on a plate. Place the sliced meat on the ratatouille with the Herb Vinaigrette on top. Add Goat Cheese Gnocchi around the edge of the plate so they don't get soggy from the sauce.

Cherry Tomato Gazpacho

Serves 6

2 pt. cherry tomatoes (or any tomato variety, color, and size),
  roughly squeezed by hand to remove most of the seeds
1 large cucumber, peeled, seeded, and roughly chopped
1 large red onion, sliced
1 red bell pepper, seeded and chopped
2 slices good-quality country white bread, crusts removed and
  roughly torn apart
3 tbsp. sugar
1 tbsp. salt
1/4 c. red wine vinegar
fresh crab meat
olive oil
squeeze of lemon juice
pinch cayenne pepper
avocado slice

Mix all of the ingredients by hand in a bowl, and let them sit for at
least 4 hours. Blend all of the ingredients in a blender till smooth.
Pass the mixture through a colander to remove any remaining
tomato seeds and skin. Chill until ready to serve. Serve garnished
with fresh crab meat, olive oil, a squeeze of lemon juice, a pinch of
cayenne, and a slice of avocado.

Warm Berry Cobbler
with Lemon Verbena Ice Cream

Serves 6

COBBLER FILLING:
- 1 pt. strawberries, stemmed and quartered
- 1 pt. blueberries
- 1 tbsp. fresh mint leaves, sliced
- 1/4 c. sugar
- 1 tbsp. cornstarch
- 1/2 vanilla bean, scraped

Mix all of the ingredients in bowl, and marinate for 1 hour or more.

COBBLER TOPPING:
- 3 1/3 c. all-purpose flour
- 1/4 c. sugar
- 2 tbsp. plus 1 tsp. baking powder
- 1/4 tsp. salt
- 12 tbsp. cold butter, diced
- 1 1/3 c. heavy cream

Place all of the ingredients except the cream in a food processer, and blend for 30 seconds. Add the cream, and blend until the mixture forms a ball. Chill for at least 1 hour. Roll into golf-ball-size balls and flatten into disks with the palm of your hand.

TO FINISH COBBLER:
- heavy cream
- raw sugar

Preheat the oven to 350 degrees. Put the fruit mixture in 6-oz. ramekins. Top each ramekin with one disk of topping. Brush with a little heavy cream, and sprinkle with raw sugar. Bake for 20 minutes or until bubbling and golden.

ICE CREAM:
- 1 1/2 c. whole milk
- 1 1/2 c. heavy cream
- 7/8 c. (or 14 tbsp.) sugar
- 1/2 c. loosely packed lemon verbena leaves
- 6 egg yolks

Combine the milk and cream, and add half of the sugar to the mixture along with the verbena leaves. Bring the mixture to a simmer. Whisk together the eggs and the remaining sugar. *Slowly* add the simmered milk mixture to the egg mixture, whisking. When everything is together, add it back to the milk pot and simmer, stirring, for another 3 to 4 minutes or until thickened enough to coat the back of a spoon. Strain through a sieve and cool completely. Freeze according to ice cream machine directions.

Every good restaurant has a story. By anyone's standards, the Grey Horse Tavern in Bayport, Long Island, has more stories than is fair. For starters, owners Linda Ringhouse and Irene Dougal named the restaurant to honor the eccentric whimsy of previous owners, who brought their gray horse into the tavern room every night to join the bar crowd for cocktails.

The Grey Horse Tavern looks not unlike your spinster aunt's sprawling mansion, which was willed to her in better times. Taking up more than an entire block, the building is an imposing and inviting three-story Victorian house adorned with enclosed porches, complete with gas stoves and overhead ceiling fans. Used year-round, each cozy side porch has a different character, depending on the season and time of day. The cavernous Tavern Room is paneled in dark wood, and the backlit, sloping stretch of bar takes up at least one-third of the room. Imagining a gray horse sidling up for a few drinks is not out of the question.

Steps away from the Tavern Room's banter and live music is the beer garden; the eyes of a gray horse statue keep watch over it, and arbor vines create a ceiling overhead.

Out back, the potager (or kitchen) gardens are four raised beds made from felled trees harvested from co-owner Irene's yard and filled with herbs, tomatoes, and vegetables, including hot cherry peppers, yellow squash, chives, and oregano, all of which help the Grey Horse Tavern's chef, Meredith Machemer, serve dishes with just-picked flavor up until late October.

Meredith didn't always know she wanted to be a chef, but she always worked in restaurants during the summers near her home in Rockville Center, Long Island. After she'd spent a year and a half in college, a friend got her a job as a pantry fry cook at Churchill's restaurant.

"I wanted to try it out, and it turned out to be an amazing experience," she says. She remembers coming home and exclaiming to her mother, "Oh my God, look! I made a sandwich."

She never attended culinary school; instead, she learned on the job from "people who loved their craft and loved to teach it," she says. She peppered the cooks with questions, and they showed her how it was done.

Her first professional cooking job was at Legal Seafood, the seafood chain that, since it was founded in 1950, has prided itself on being a "fish company in the restaurant business." She worked at Legal Seafood for almost five years, absorbing its pier-to-plate philosophy. Meredith says the cooks at Legal Seafood, including local farm-to-table pioneer Chef Stephen Cardello, turned out consistent-quality meals working with only seasonal, sustainable fish.

When Cardello discovered the Grey Horse Tavern's sixty-five-seat restaurant and showed Meredith its farm-inspired menu, she remembers being jealous of what she saw as its cooks' creativity and freedom of food expression. Ringhouse and Dougal were visionaries, she thought, because they posted their mission statement on the menu, promising to serve local farm fresh food. They served only humanely raised meat and supported local farmers and artisans. They listed all their farmers, fishermen, and dairy names and locations on the menu too.

When Cardello took over as Grey Horse Tavern's executive chef, Meredith joined him as his sous chef. When he left a year later, she took over the executive chef reins.

Today, Meredith maintains the relationships with local growers that she established when she first accompanied Cardello to the Grey Horse Tavern, including Satur Farms, Catapano Dairy Farm, the Fish Store, and Braun's Fish Market. Main Street Meats is the local butcher in Farmingdale, and ranchers connected with gourmet-food supplier D'Artagnan provide only grass-fed beef.

Meredith, Ringside, and Dougal consistently seek out quality local-food sources.

"On Thursdays, I go out to the Organics Today Farm in Islip to get the melons, eggplants, broccolini, swiss chard, and heirloom tomatoes, for example," Meredith says. "In the spring, Irene and I volunteer at the farm to help plant."

As the Grey Horse Tavern's reputation for serving fresh, local, and sustainable food spreads, more and more of the South Shore's small farmers and producers are stopping in to do business. Meredith comes up with menu ideas when she sees what's available and fresh at the markets.

"I see things there or in the garden that I can't wait to use," she says. "Most times, I'm working with flavors rather than trying to follow from a written recipe."

Because of the restaurant's tavern style and the fact that it offers live music, many guests come to the Grey Horse Tavern several times a week. While that kind of customer loyalty is enviable, it challenges Meredith to keep the menu consistently basic but different.

"You can't bore your customers nor alienate them with things they don't know or think they won't like," she says. But she's also committed to persuading customers to enjoy the changing, seasonal menus.

For her part, hands-on chef Meredith is excited that every day she continues to learn on the job. She respects the ingredients and believes in keeping the food simple.

"When I'm working in the kitchen and need to eat, I love putting something wonderfully delicious on two pieces of bread," she says. "I can still make a very cool sandwich! And that's something."

Local Peach and Organic Beefsteak Tomato Salad

Serves 4–6

1 1/2 c. plain goat's milk yogurt (preferably from Catapano Dairy Farm)
1/4 c. local honey
kosher salt and freshly ground black pepper, to taste
3 peaches
4 medium Beefsteak tomatoes
4 heads lollo rosso, rinsed and dried
1 (4.5 oz.) package chevre, pulled apart into pieces (preferably from Catapano Dairy Farm)
6 leaves fresh basil, cut chiffonade

Whisk the yogurt and honey together, and season with salt and pepper. Adjust as desired. Set aside. Halve and pit the peaches, and cut them into thick wedges. Thickly slice the tomatoes. Separate the lettuce leaves.

On a large platter, lay the tomato slices out along the edge of the dish. Season with salt and pepper. Layer the peach slices and lettuce over the tomatoes. Drizzle with yogurt dressing and top with chevre. Drizzle more dressing over the top of the salad. (You won't use all of the dressing. Serve extra on the side, if needed.) Distribute the basil leaves evenly over the top of the salad. Serve immediately.

Linguine with Local Clams, Rainbow Swiss Chard, and Broccolini

Serves 4

1/2 lb. pancetta, cut into 1/4-inch cubes

5 medium garlic cloves, thinly sliced

3 tbsp. shallots, minced

1/2 c. dry white wine

3 dozen local littleneck clams, scrubbed and soaked in several changes of cold water

2 bunches broccolini, blanched and roughly chopped

2 bunches rainbow swiss chard, stems removed and chopped, leaves torn

4 tbsp. unsalted butter

kosher salt and freshly ground black pepper, to taste

1 lb. fresh linguine

1 c. Parmesan Reggiano, shaved

Heat a large, heavy-bottomed pot on high heat. Put the pancetta in, and cook until it is brown and crispy. Remove the pancetta from the pot with a slotted spoon, and drain on a paper towel. Reserve 1/2 c. of the pancetta liquid, and sauté the garlic until it starts to brown on the edges. Add the shallots. Sauté shallots until translucent and deglaze with white wine, making sure to scrape the bottom of the pot to loosen any extra brown bits from the pan. Add the littlenecks, and cover the pot with a tight-fitting lid. Check the pot to make sure all of the clams have opened; once they have, remove the clams with tongs and set them aside. Turn the heat down to medium, and add the broccolini and Swiss chard. Cook until the Swiss chard is wilted but not browning. Add the butter. Do not boil. Season to taste with salt and pepper.

Meanwhile, bring a large pot of salted water to a boil. Once the water is boiling, cook the linguine until it's al dente (around 8 to 10 minutes). Drain the linguine in a colander, and separate it into four large pasta bowls.

Divide the Swiss chard and broccolini mixture on top of each bowl of linguine. Place the clams around the edges of the bowl, and sprinkle each dish with the pancetta and a generous amount of shaved Parmesan Reggiano. Serve immediately.

Pan-Seared Local Scallops with Summer Succotash, Frisée Salad, and Crispy Fried Beets

Serves 4

SUMMER SUCCOTASH:

4 ears local bicolor corn, husks on

1/2 red onion, thinly sliced

2 cloves garlic, minced

6 cherry peppers, seeded and thinly sliced

kosher salt and fresh ground black pepper, to taste

1/4 c. dry white wine

1/2 lb. haricot verts, cleaned, blanched, and cut into
  1/2-inch pieces

1/2 lb. yellow wax beans, cleaned, blanched, and cut into
  1/2-inch pieces

1 pt. heirloom cherry tomatoes, halved

1–1 1/2 c. organic heavy cream

1/4–1/2 c. Parmesan Reggiano, freshly grated

2 tbsp. unsalted butter

6 leaves of fresh basil, cut chiffonade

Soak the corn in a pot of cold water for 15 minutes. Shake off excess water, and cook on heated grill plate. Grill the corn until the outer leaves are browned and slightly charred. Set aside.

When the corn has cooled slightly, remove the husk and cut the kernels off the cob. (Reserve the cobs for stock for a later use.) Set the kernels aside.

In a large sauté pan on medium-high heat, sauté the onions until they are translucent. Do not brown the onions. Add the garlic and cherry peppers, and season with salt and pepper. Once the peppers are starting to soften, deglaze with white wine and reduce until almost no wine is left. Add the corn, haricot verts, wax beans, and cherry tomatoes. Sauté until almost heated through (about 1 minute). Add the heavy cream and Parmesan cheese, and lower heat to medium. Reduce the heavy cream until sauce is slightly thick. Season with salt and pepper.

Add the butter and the basil. Stir to incorporate the butter.

SCALLOPS:

1/4 c grapeseed oil

2 lb. sea scallops

kosher salt and freshly ground black pepper, to taste

While the succotash cream is reducing, heat a large cast-iron skillet with grapeseed oil on high. Season the scallops with salt and pepper. Just as the oil starts to smoke, add the scallops, making sure not to crowd the pan. (You may have to cook the scallops in batches.) Don't flip the scallops until they have a nice brown caramelized sear. Once the scallops are ready to be flipped, turn the heat to medium low and cook for 1 to 2 minutes. Take scallops out of the pan, and drain on a paper towel.

FRISÉE SALAD:

1/2 c. grapeseed oil

4–6 baby beets, peeled and sliced thinly on the mandoline

kosher salt and freshly ground black pepper

3–4 tbsp. Spanish olive oil

1 tbsp. local honey

2 small heads of frisée lettuce

Fill a medium-sized pot with about 1 inch of grapeseed oil over high heat. Once the oil is hot enough (a water droplet will crackle when oil is ready), drop the beet slices into the oil and cook 3 to 4 minutes, until crispy. Remove the beets from the oil with a slotted spoon, and drain on a paper towel. Season with kosher salt.

In a small bowl, whisk together the olive oil and honey. Tear the frisée, and add it to the bowl. Season with salt and pepper. Set aside.

To serve: Divide the Summer Succotash onto the center of four separate plates. Divide the scallops, evenly placing them on top of the succotash. Top the scallops with the Frisée Salad, and finish with the crispy fried beets. Serve immediately.

Pan-Seared Local Scallops

with Summer Succotash, Frisée Salad, and Crispy Fried Beets

Restaurant Directory

18 Bay
23 North Ferry Road
Shelter Island, NY 11964
(631) 749-0053
www.18bayrestaurant.com

1770 House
143 Main Street
East Hampton, NY 11937
(631) 324-1770
www.1770house.com

Almond
One Ocean Road
Bridgehampton, NY 11932
(631) 537-5665
www.almondrestaurant.com

Amarelle Restaurant
2028 North Country Rd
Wading River, NY 11792
(631) 886-2242
www.amarelle.net

The American Hotel
Main Street
Sag Harbor, NY
(631) 725-3535
www.theamericanhotel.com

CoolFish
6800 Jericho Turnpike
Syosset, NY 11791
(516) 921-3250
www.tomschaudel.com

Cuvée Bistro & Bar, Greenporter Hotel
326 Front Street
Greenport, NY 11944
(631) 477-0066
www.greenporterhotel.com

East Hampton Grill (formerly Della Femina)
136 North Main Street
East Hampton, NY 11937
(631) 329-6660

Foody's
760 Montauk Highway
Water Mill, NY 11976
(631) 726-FOOD (3663)

Fresno
8 Fresno Place
East Hampton, NY 11937
(631) 324-8700
www.fresnorestaurant.com

The Frisky Oyster
27 Front Street
Greenport, NY 11944
(631) 477-4265
www.thefriskyoyster.com

The Grey Horse Tavern
291 Bayport Avenue
Bayport, NY 11705
(631) 472-1868
www.greyhorsetavern.com

Jedediah Hawkins Inn
400 South Jamesport Avenue
Jamesport, NY 11947
(631) 772-2900
www.jedediahhawkinsinn.com

Kitchen A Bistro
404 N. Country Rd
St. James, NY 11780
(631) 862-0151
www.kitchenabistro.com

Kitchen A Trattoria
532 North Country Road
St. James, NY 11780
(631) 584-3518

The Lake House
240 West Main Street
Bayshore, NY 11706
(631) 666-0995
www.thelakehouserest.com

The Living Room at the Maidstone Hotel
207 Main Street
East Hampton, NY 11937
(631) 324-5006
www.careofhotels.com/maidstone

Loaves & Fishes
50 Sagg Main Street
Sagaponack, NY 11962
(631) 537-0555
www.landfcookshop.com

Mitch & Toni's American Bistro
875 Willis Avenue
Albertson, NY 11507
(516) 741-7940
www.mitchandtonis.com

Nick & Toni's
136 North Main Street
East Hampton, NY 11937
(631) 324-3550
www.nickandtonis.com

North Fork Table & Inn
57225 Main Road
Southold, NY 11971
(631) 765-0177
www.northforktableandinn.com

Restaurant Mirabelle
150 Main Street
Stony Brook, New York 11790
(631) 751-0555
www.threevillageinn.com

Satur Farms
3705 Allvah's Lane
Cutchogue, NY 11935
(631) 734-4219
www.saturfarms.com

Scrimshaw
102 Main Street
Greenport, NY 11944
(631) 477-8882
www.scrimshawrestaurant.com

Southfork Kitchen
203 Sag Harbor Turnpike
Bridgehampton, NY 11932
(631) 537-4700
www.southforkkitchen.com

Starr Boggs
6 Parlato Drive
Westhampton, NY 11978
(631) 288-3500
www.starrboggsrestaurant.com

Swallow
366 New York Avenue
Huntington, NY
(631) 547-5388
www.swallowrestaurant.com

Vine Street Café
41 South Ferry Road
Shelter Island, NY 11964
(631) 749-3210
www.vinestreetcafe.com

About the Author and Photographers

For more than a decade, **Leeann Lavin** worked in communications at Brooklyn Botanic Garden and the New York Botanical Garden before becoming an award-winning garden designer with Duchess Designs, LLC. Leeann's reviews about gardens and chefs have appeared in the *Wall Street Journal*, on *Food & Drink*, and on her blog, celebritychefsandtheirgardens.blogspot.com.

Photographer and artist **Lindsay Morris** spent a decade working in fine art photography before branching out to design her own line of women's clothing. In 2006, she made her way back to her original passion and has held the position of photo editor of *Edible East End* magazine for the past five years.

Jennifer Calais Smith, a New York City–based photographer specializing in architecture, food, gardens, travel, and interiors has been published in *Architectural Record*, *Town & Country*, and *Metropolis*, as well as on foodandwine.com, among others.

Author Leeann Lavin

Acknowledgments

This book would not have been possible without the support of family and friends. I am especially grateful to my father, George, who I wish had lived long enough to see the book. Special thanks to my mother, Virginia, a kitchen wizard whose baking gives credence to the cultural idiom "as good as Mom's apple pie." My grandfather, Michael, taught me to dig potatoes in the garden, which was like hunting for buried treasure. The chore left a happy memory that inspires my edible gardening.

I thank Bill for his love, patience, and forbearance as well as for his creative opinions—from the book's concept to the rigors of writing to the dodgy scheduling of photo shoots. And along the way he became a master chef and gardener! I am also grateful to my talented cousin, Maryann DeLeo, for her thoughtful reading of the profiles.

I am particularly beholden to the talented chefs and their inspired growers. It wasn't enough that each chosen chef be a good cook; that was a given. Rather, the chefs had be visionaries who had long held a passion for using locally nurtured food ingredients. And I would be remiss if I didn't thank the legions of restaurant goers who loyally eat at these homegrown chefs' tables, allowing them to lead incredibly delicious food explorations.

I am indebted to photographers Lindsay Morris and Jennifer Calais Smith. I asked that the images tell stories, showcase unique talents, and render a sense of place, and they succeeded brilliantly. Lindsay, your name alone is currency with the chefs and growers, and your *Edible East End* photography will surely earn a James Beard award.

I thank my friends, Roberta and Mary Kay, for everything and my Tannin girlfriends for their unflagging encouragement. I also gratefully acknowledge my longtime garden design clients, especially Joseph DiMattina. I salute Uncle Bob's wisdom, and Maria Steinberg is a garden angel, master cook, cheerleader, and guide.

I gratefully acknowledge my editors: Hannah, for giving me the confidence to pursue the concept; Kari Cornell, for her insight and vision to see the proposal as a series; and Melinda Keefe, for her superb management, keen style, and communication skills. You're a dream, Melinda—thank you so very much.

Finally, I thank everyone who helped make the book a fitting tribute to nature's inspiration for artists—all artists, but especially culinary artists because they use the garden's bounty in their creations. I have sought to honor their work.

—Leeann Lavin

Index

First published in 2012 by Voyageur Press, an imprint of MBI Publishing Company, 400 First Avenue North, Suite 300, Minneapolis, MN 55401 USA

© 2012 Voyageur Press, an imprint of MBI Publishing Company LLC
Text © 2012 Leeann Lavin
Photography © 2012 Lindsay Morris and Jennifer Calais Smith
All photographs are from the author's collection unless noted otherwise.
Title page: © Len Holsborg/Alamy

From Getty Images: Cover top inset: © Skip Brown/National Geographic/Getty Images, cover center inset: © Agencja Free/GAP Photos/Getty Images, p. 65: © Rita Maas/FoodPix

From Shutterstock.com: p. 30 and back cover inset: © Jiang Hongyan, p. 31: © Lilyana Vynogradova, p. 34: © Anna Hoychuk, p. 35: © Susan Fox, p. 41: © Francesco83, p. 55: © Barbara Dudzinska, p. 64: © Dream79, p. 74: © Phloen, p. 75: © M Ishikawa, p. 78: © Lasse Kristensen, p. 90: © Rihardzz, p. 101: © Jacques PALUT, p. 118: © Geoff Hardy, p. 123: © Bryan Solomon, p. 137: © Matka Wariatka, p. 153: © Tanya Emsh

The information in this book is true and complete to the best of our knowledge. All recommendations are made without any guarantee on the part of the author or Publisher, who also disclaims any liability incurred in connection with the use of this data or specific details.

We recognize, further, that some words, model names, and designations mentioned herein are the property of the trademark holder. We use them for identification purposes only. This is not an official publication.

Voyageur Press titles are also available at discounts in bulk quantity for industrial or sales-promotional use. For details write to Special Sales Manager at MBI Publishing Company, 400 First Avenue North, Suite 300, Minneapolis, MN 55401 USA.

To find out more about our books, visit us online at www.voyageurpress.com.

ISBN-13: 978-0-7603-3757-8

Library of Congress Cataloging-in-Publication Data

Lavin, Leeann, 1955-
The Hamptons and Long Island homegrown cookbook : local food, local chefs, local
recipes / Leeann Lavin ; photographs by Jennifer Calais Smith and Lindsay Morris. -- 1st ed.
     p. cm.
  ISBN 978-0-7603-3757-8 (plc w/ jkt)
 1. Cooking, American. 2. Cooking--New York (State)--Long Island. 3.
Restaurants--New York (State)--Long Island. 4. Cookbooks. I. Title.
 TX715.L367 2011
 641.59747'21--dc22
                              2010053616

Editor: Melinda Keefe
Design Manager: Cindy Samargia Laun
Series designed by: Ellen Huber
Layout by: Pauline Molinari
Cover designed by: Karl Laun

Printed in China

10 9 8 7 6 5 4 3 2 1